读故事
巧记 KET 核心词汇

土豆教育 / 组编　刘薇 / 编著

本书以KET官方词表为基础，将KET核心词汇（1500余词）整合为14个场景，设置为28天的学习任务。每天包含以下四个部分：1. 基础词汇回顾；2. 情景故事（搭配"故事导读"和"参考译文"）；3. 词汇讲解；4. 词汇练习。

"基础词汇回顾"帮助学生复习基础词汇；"情景故事"以生动有趣的小故事串联每天需要掌握的KET核心词汇，让学生置身于情景中学习词汇，并掌握词汇在语句中的具体运用；"词汇讲解"从多角度解读单词，辅助学生记忆；"词汇练习"贴近真题题型，将听、说、读、写充分融入练习之中，所练即所考，能帮助学生在记忆核心词汇的同时熟悉KET真题题型及考点，进而实现快速提分。

图书在版编目（CIP）数据

读故事：巧记KET核心词汇／土豆教育组编；刘薇编著. —北京：机械工业出版社，2021.1（2025.7重印）
ISBN 978－7－111－67196－1

Ⅰ.①读… Ⅱ.①土… ②刘… Ⅲ.①英语水平考试－词汇-自学参考资料 Ⅳ.①H313

中国版本图书馆CIP数据核字（2020）第266954号

机械工业出版社（北京市百万庄大街22号　邮政编码100037）
策划编辑：尹小云　　责任编辑：尹小云
责任校对：张若男　　责任印制：张　博
三河市宏达印刷有限公司印刷
2025年7月第1版第34次印刷
184mm×260mm·12.5印张·276千字
标准书号：ISBN 978－7－111－67196－1
定价：48.00元

电话服务　　　　　　　　网络服务
客服电话：010－88361066　机　工　官　网：www.cmpbook.com
　　　　　010－88379833　机　工　官　博：weibo.com/cmp1952
　　　　　010－68326294　金　书　网：www.golden-book.com
封底无防伪标均为盗版　　　机工教育服务网：www.cmpedu.com

编委会

主任委员 刘 薇
副主任委员 赵 健　刘炜丽　张美燕
委　　员 马 敏　王 娟　尹星钰
　　　　　　杨文明　卢芳惠　彭 琳

前 言
Preface

"剑桥通用英语考试"(MSE,Main Suite Examinations)是由剑桥大学英语考评部设立,由中国教育部考试中心引进的一项英语水平考试。该考试从听力、口语、写作、阅读四个部分对考生的英语水平进行综合性考查。考试合格者将获得由英国剑桥大学考试委员会颁发的证书。该考试从低到高共分为五个级别,分别是:

入门水平:英语入门考试(KET考试,全称Key English Test)
初级水平:初级英语考试(PET考试,全称Preliminary English Test)
独立水平:第一英语证书考试(FCE考试,全称First Certificate in English)
流利运用:高级英语证书考试(CAE考试,全称Certificate in Advanced English)
熟练运用:熟练英语证书考试(CPE考试,全称Certificate of Proficiency in English)

MSE考试的试题与阅卷均由拥有丰富英语教学经验的专家团队完成,能为英语学习者提供阶段性、系统性的测评。KET考试为MSE考试五个级别中的第一级,它是一项基础英语水平认证,通过该考试的考生能够与以英语为母语或非母语的人士就日常生活、旅游及学习等熟悉话题进行简单的对话交流,拥有良好的英语基础。KET考试能真实地反映考生听、说、读、写四个部分的水平,能为调整语言学习目标提供参考,也能为考生后续挑战PET等一系列进阶考试打下基础。

近年来,MSE考试公正公平、权威性强、含金量高、适用范围广等一系列优点吸引了广大学生和家长的目光,热度不断提升,其中的KET考试已经成为青少年迈向更高英语学习层次的必经之路。

为了顺利通过KET考试,取得证书,学生需要拥有基础英语能力。而熟练掌握词汇是踏实有效地提升英语能力的第一步,也是最为关键的一步。为了帮助考生更好地掌握KET考试核心词汇,切实提高英语水平,取得理想的考试成绩,我们编写了《读故事 巧记KET核心词汇》一书。

本书特色如下:

科学规划,核心词汇一网打尽

本书参考最新版官方词表,收录KET考试核心词汇共1500余个。全书按照科学的记忆习惯编排,设置了28天的学习任务,能有效提升学生的词汇量。每个单元学习内容开始前提供学前测试,可供学生自测,提前了解词汇掌握情况,以提升学习效率,做到事半功倍。

情景故事，趣味性强，寓教于乐

  KET 考试的话题多与各类生活场景息息相关，因此本书共设置 14 个单元，每单元两组主题词汇，用这 28 组词汇串联成一个个生动有趣的情景故事，并由英语专家朗读。将单词植入语境，让学生在情景中学习，能让其越学越有兴趣和动力。在确保趣味性的同时，本书兼具专业性。核心词汇均配有精准的中文释义和音标，并提供例句、常用搭配、联想、助记等拓展，帮助学生在记忆单词的同时，充分领会单词的含义和用法，并且能够更准确灵活地应用单词。

真题模拟，知识要点随记随测

  要学更要练！每天的学习内容后都附有自主练习题，学生可以随学、随记、随练，及时查漏补缺，检验学习成果。将真题题型融入日常练习中，能帮助学生加强词汇记忆，做到学习效果最大化。同时，练习题后均附有答案，便于学生自检或者家长辅助学习。

听说读写，英语能力全面提升

  自主练习题涵盖单元核心词汇，围绕听、说、读、写四大板块设置。题型丰富多变，模拟 KET 考试真题编写，针对性强，难度适中，可为学生提前适应 KET 考试的题目设计和答题思路打下基础，锻炼学生的英语思维能力。

  我们希望通过《读故事 巧记 KET 核心词汇》以及进阶的《读故事 巧记 PET 核心词汇》，给学生带来更富有趣味性的英语学习体验，帮助学生轻松记单词，打好英语基础，并激发学生对英语学习的热情和兴趣。最后，预祝使用本书的考生们能顺利通过考试，取得优异的成绩，在英语学习的道路上有所收获！

编　者

使用说明

听音频，自测主题词汇

Pre-test

快速浏览下面的单词，自测一下，看看你是否已经掌握了呢？记得标记你不熟悉的单词，多多复习哦！

- ☐ child [tʃaɪld] n. 儿童；小孩
- ☐ pen-friend n. 笔友
- ☐ son [sʌn] n. 儿子
- ☐ grandson [ˈɡrænsʌn] n. 孙子；外孙
- ☐ grandchild [ˈɡræntʃaɪld] n.（外）孙子；（外）孙女
- ☐ boyfriend [ˈbɔɪfrend] n. 男朋友
- ☐ girlfriend [ˈɡɜːlfrend] n. 女朋友
- ☐ name [neɪm] n. 名字；名称
- ☐ first name 名字
- ☐ surname [ˈsɜːneɪm] n.

了解需要掌握的词汇

Day 1

故事导读：
1. 小朋友，试着在故事中找找 Judy 有哪些家人吧；
2. 拿起笔圈出自己还不熟悉的单词吧。

Reading

听音频，读故事，在趣味情景中学习词汇

Judy Hopper is a cute bunny. She lives with her parents and her brother Peter.

One day, Judy's father, Mr Hopper received a letter from his older sister.

"Dear brother, my daughter Fluffy is getting married in August! She and your aunt Anna and uncle Steve want Judy and Peter to be the flower girl and page boy (花童)." Mr

对照译文，理解、复习词汇，或检查词汇掌握情况

参考译文

朱迪

朱迪·霍珀是一只可爱的小兔子，她和爸爸妈妈以及弟弟彼得一起住在一片美丽的森林里。

一天，朱迪的爸爸霍珀先生收到了一封来自他姐姐的信。

"亲爱的弟弟，我的女儿弗拉想让朱迪和彼得当当花童。"霍珀先生……

"哇！我等不及要去参加婚礼见到爷爷奶奶和其他家庭成员了。"……

Exercise

I. Listen and read the phrases aloud.

1. father and mother
2. daddy and mummy
3. brother and sister
4. boy and girl
5. husband and wife
6. uncle and aunt
7. Mr and Mrs
8. grandfather and grandmother
9. grandson and granddaughter

听音频并跟读，模拟标准口语发音

Word list

听音频，学习标准发音

parent [ˈpeərənt] n. 父亲（或母亲）
注意 常用其复数形式 parents。
例句 Children need their parents. 孩子们需要父母。

brother [ˈbrʌðə(r)] n. 兄；弟

a younger sister 妹妹
dear [dɪə(r)] adj. 亲爱的
daughter [ˈdɔːtə(r)] n. 女儿
married [ˈmærɪd] adj. 已婚的

掌握核心词汇的用法

II. Label your family members.

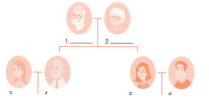

多种形式的练习题帮助学生熟记和运用 KET 词汇

III. Listen and fill in the blanks. Write one word or a number for each blank.

Emma's Birthday Party Plan
When: next Saturday
Where: at Mr and Mrs Haywood's house
Number of guests: 1. _____
Preparation: a chocolate cake, flowers, candles, and 2. _____
Mr Hay...

新版 KET 听力题型，提供听力原文和音频，帮助学生提前适应题目设计和答题思路

IV. Answer the questions.

1. How many people are there in y...
   _____
   _____
2. Who are they?
   _____

运用主题词汇写句子，循序渐进训练写作能力

IV. Read the email from your pen-friend, Andy.

From:	Andy
To:	

Hello! It's nice to know you. My name is Andy and I'm ten years old. I live in New York. What about you? How many people are there in your family? Do you have good friends?

IV. Look at the three pictures.

Write the story shown in the pictures.
Write 35 words or more.

新版 KET 写作题型，提供标准参考范文，让学生提前适应考题和答题方法

目 录

Contents

前言

使用说明

Unit 1　Family and Friends / 001
    Day 1　/ 003
    Day 2　/ 008

Unit 2　House and Home / 013
    Day 3　/ 015
    Day 4　/ 020

Unit 3　Education / 025
    Day 5　/ 027
    Day 6　/ 032

Unit 4　Shopping and Clothes / 037
    Day 7　/ 039
    Day 8　/ 044

Unit 5　Food and Drink / 049
    Day 9　/ 051
    Day 10　/ 056

Unit 6　Sport / 061
    Day 11　/ 063
    Day 12　/ 069

Unit 7　Hobbies and Jobs / 075
    Day 13　/ 077
    Day 14　/ 082

Unit 8　Places and Buildings / 087
    Day 15　/ 089
    Day 16　/ 094

Unit 9　Technology / 099
    Day 17　/ 101
    Day 18　/ 106

Unit 10　Time, Colour, Weather and Nature / 111
    Day 19　/ 113
    Day 20　/ 119

Unit 11　Invitation / 125
    Day 21　/ 127
    Day 22　/ 132

Unit 12　Health, Medicine and Exercise / 137
    Day 23　/ 139
    Day 24　/ 144

Unit 13　Travel and Transport / 149
    Day 25　/ 151
    Day 26　/ 156

Unit 14　Communication / 161
    Day 27　/ 163
    Day 28　/ 169

参考答案　/ 174

Unit 1
Family and Friends

Pre-test

快速浏览下面的单词，自测一下，看看你是否已经掌握了呢？记得标记你不熟悉的单词，多多复习哦！

- [ ] child [tʃaɪld] *n.* 儿童；小孩
- [ ] pen-friend *n.* 笔友
- [ ] son [sʌn] *n.* 儿子
- [ ] grandson ['grænsʌn] *n.* 孙子；外孙
- [ ] grandchild ['græntʃaɪld] *n.* （外）孙子；（外）孙女
- [ ] boyfriend ['bɔɪfrend] *n.* 男朋友
- [ ] girlfriend ['gɜːlfrend] *n.* 女朋友
- [ ] name [neɪm] *n.* 名字；名称
- [ ] first name 名字
- [ ] surname ['sɜːneɪm] *n.* 姓
- [ ] Mr ['mɪstə(r)] 先生
- [ ] Ms [mɪz] 女士
- [ ] Mrs ['mɪsɪz] 太太，夫人
- [ ] Miss [mɪs] 小姐，女士
- [ ] age [eɪdʒ] *n.* 年龄
- [ ] aged [eɪdʒd] *adj.* ……岁 ['eɪdʒɪd] *adj.* 年迈的
- [ ] born [bɔːn] *v.* （仅用于被动语态）出生；出世
- [ ] once [wʌns] *adv.* 一次
- [ ] twice [twaɪs] *adv.* 两次；两遍
- [ ] sometimes ['sʌmtaɪmz] *adv.* 有时；间或
- [ ] all the time 始终，一直
- [ ] birth [bɜːθ] *n.* 出生；诞生
- [ ] never ['nevə(r)] *adv.* 从不；绝不
- [ ] often ['ɒfn] *adv.* 时常；常常
- [ ] usual ['juːʒuəl] *adj.* 通常的；惯常的
- [ ] usually ['juːʒuəli] *adv.* 通常地
- [ ] each [iːtʃ] *det. & pron.* 各个，每个
- [ ] every ['evri] *det.* 每一个，每个
- [ ] exciting [ɪk'saɪtɪŋ] *adj.* 令人激动的；使人兴奋的

故事导读：
1. 小朋友，试着在故事中找找Judy有哪些家人吧；
2. 拿起笔圈出自己还不熟悉的单词吧。

Judy

Judy Hopper is a cute bunny who lives in a beautiful forest with her parents and her brother Peter.

One day, Judy's father, Mr Hopper received a letter from his older sister.

"Dear brother, my daughter Fluffy is getting married in August! She and your aunt Anna and uncle Steve want Judy and Peter to be the flower girl and page boy(花童)." Mr Hopper put on his glasses and read.

"Yay! I can't wait to go to my cousin's wedding(婚礼)!" Judy was so happy and jumped high. She hadn't seen her grandparents and other family members for a long time. "Mummy, can I have a new dress?" she asked.

"Of course," answered her mother cheerfully.

The wedding took place in a white church by a lake. Judy was in her new pink dress and Peter was in his new smart suit. Along with music, they walked into the venue with two pretty flower baskets.

"I like your cute dress." Grandmother whispered to her granddaughter when she sat down beside her.

Judy gave Grandmother a big smile.

"I now pronounce(宣布) you husband and wife," said Father Rabbit. All the guests burst into applause(掌声) for the couple in love.

The family and friends sang and danced happily until the moon and stars came out.

"I like everyone's smiling and laughing," Judy told her father before she fell asleep. Then she had the sweetest dream ever.

朱迪

参考译文

朱迪·霍珀是一只可爱的小兔子，她和爸爸妈妈以及弟弟彼得一起住在一片美丽的森林里。

一天，朱迪的爸爸霍珀先生收到了一封来自他姐姐的信。

"亲爱的弟弟，我的女儿弗拉菲将在八月份结婚！她和你的安娜婶婶、史蒂夫叔叔想让朱迪和彼得当花童。"霍珀先生戴上眼镜念道。

"哇！我等不及要去参加表姐的婚礼了！"朱迪开心地蹦了起来。她已经很久没有见到爷爷奶奶和其他家庭成员了。"妈妈，我可以穿一条新裙子吗？"她问道。

"当然可以了。"霍珀太太愉快地回答道。

婚礼在湖畔的一座白色教堂里举行。朱迪穿着她粉红色的新裙子，彼得穿着他漂亮的新西装。伴随着音乐，他们挎着两个漂亮的花篮走进了教堂。

"我喜欢你的漂亮裙子。"奶奶在孙女身旁坐下时小声地对她说。

朱迪向奶奶露出了一个大大的笑容。

"我现在宣布你们正式结为夫妻。"兔子神父说。所有的宾客都为这对沉浸在爱情中的新人报以热烈的掌声。

家人和朋友们快乐地唱歌跳舞，直到月亮和星星出来了。

"我喜欢每个人的欢声笑语。"朱迪在入睡前对爸爸说。然后，她做了一个最甜美的梦。

parent [ˈpeərənt] n. 父亲（或母亲）
注意 常用其复数形式 parents。
例句 Children need their parents. 孩子们需要父母。

brother [ˈbrʌðə(r)] n. 兄；弟
搭配 an older brother 哥哥
　　　a younger brother 弟弟

father [ˈfɑːðə(r)] n. 父亲；爸爸

old [əʊld] adj. 老的；年纪大的（比较级：older）

sister [ˈsɪstə(r)] n. 姐；妹
搭配 an older sister 姐姐
　　　a younger sister 妹妹

dear [dɪə(r)] adj. 亲爱的

daughter [ˈdɔːtə(r)] n. 女儿

married [ˈmærid] adj. 已婚的
搭配 get married 结婚

aunt [ɑːnt] n. 姑母；姨母；伯母；婶母；舅母

uncle [ˈʌŋkl] n. 舅父；叔父；伯父；姑父；姨父

flower [ˈflaʊə(r)] n. 花；花朵

girl [ɡɜːl] n. 女孩；姑娘

Day 1

搭配 a flower girl 女花童
a little girl of six 六岁的小女孩

boy [bɔɪ] *n.* 男孩
例句 He was still a little boy. 他还是个小男孩。
搭配 a page boy 男花童

put on 穿上，戴上

glasses [ˈɡlɑːsɪz] *n.* 眼镜
注意 glasses 是 glass 的复数形式。
搭配 put on a pair of glasses 戴上一副眼镜

cousin [ˈkʌzn] *n.* 堂（表）兄弟姐妹
例句 She's my cousin. 她是我的表妹。

happy [ˈhæpi] *adj.* 快乐的；高兴的
反义 unhappy 不开心的

grandparent [ˈɡrænpeərənt] *n.* 祖父；祖母；外祖父；外祖母
注意 常用其复数形式 grandparents。

family [ˈfæməli] *n.* 家人；家庭
搭配 a family of four 四口之家

member [ˈmembə(r)] *n.* 成员
搭配 a family member 家庭成员

mummy [ˈmʌmi] *n.* （尤作儿语）妈咪

mother [ˈmʌðə(r)] *n.* 母亲；妈妈

grandmother [ˈɡrænmʌðə(r)] *n.* 祖母；外祖母

granddaughter [ˈɡrændɔːtə(r)] *n.* 孙女；外孙女

husband [ˈhʌzbənd] *n.* 丈夫

wife [waɪf] *n.* 妻子；太太（*pl.* wives）
搭配 husband and wife 夫妇

guest [ɡest] *n.* 客人；宾客
搭配 wedding guests 出席婚礼的宾客

love [lʌv] *n. & v.* 爱；热爱
搭配 a mother's love for her children 母亲对孩子的爱
例句 I love you. 我爱你。

friend [frend] *n.* 朋友；友人
搭配 an old friend 老朋友 a close friend 密友

everyone [ˈevriwʌn] *pron.* 每人；人人；所有人
同义 everybody 每人

dream [driːm] *n.* 梦 *v.* 做梦
例句 Goodnight. Sweet dreams. 晚安。祝你做个好梦。

Exercise

1. Listen and read the phrases aloud.

1. father and mother
2. daddy and mummy
3. brother and sister
4. boy and girl
5. husband and wife
6. uncle and aunt
7. Mr and Mrs
8. grandfather and grandmother
9. grandson and granddaughter

II. Label your family members.

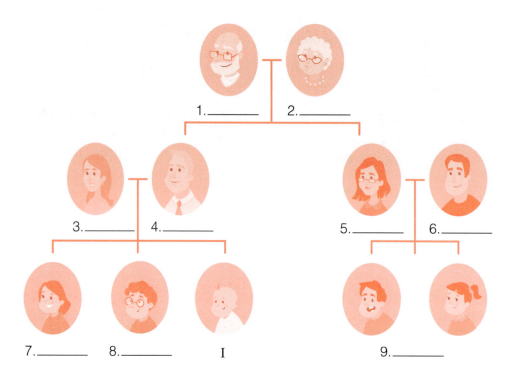

III. Listen and choose the correct answer for each question.

1. Which is John's family?

A   B

2. Who is doing the homework?

A   B

3. Who will come to visit Lucy's family on Friday?

A   B

IV. Answer the questions.

1. How many people are there in your family?

_____

_____

2. Who are they?

_____

_____

3. Do you love your family?

_____

_____

故事导读：
1. 小朋友，你是否像Emma一样收到过家人和朋友准备的惊喜礼物呢？
2. 记得标记出新学到的单词和句式哦。

Emma's Birthday Party

Emma Haywood is a seventh-grade girl with blonde hair who lives in a small seaside town. She is always friendly to others. Years ago, she became interested in sailing. Afterwards, she was allowed to take part in a competition and won first prize.

Last Saturday was Emma's 13th birthday. Her parents decided to hold a surprise party for Emma, who would be a teenager. They asked her best friends John and Harriet, who are also their neighbours, for help.

"John, could you give Emma a call and ask her to go to the beach on Saturday morning?" asked Mr Haywood on the phone. "After she leaves the house, Harriet will come and help us with the cake and balloons."

"Certainly!" John answered in an excited voice.

On that day, Emma came back home and she was so surprised and happy to hear all her family and friends shouting out "Happy birthday!" and singing a birthday song for her.

"It's time for you to make a wish, my kid." Mrs Haywood showed up with a chocolate cake and gently kissed her forehead.

"First thank you all for coming here." Emma looked at everyone with a smile. "Now it's time for my wish."

"I hope my dream of being an Olympic champion will come true," thought Emma, with her eyes closed and hands folded. Then she blew out all the candles.

Emma's parents and friends gave her many lovely gifts. They enjoyed the food and played games together happily for the whole afternoon.

"What an interesting day! It is my best birthday memory," wrote Emma in her diary.

艾玛的生日派对

艾玛·海伍德是一名有着金色头发的七年级女生,她住在一个海边小镇上。她对别人总是非常友善。几年前,她对帆船运动产生了兴趣。后来,她被允许参加比赛,并获得了一等奖。

上周六是艾玛的13岁生日。她的父母决定为即将成为青少年的艾玛举办一个惊喜派对。他们向她最好的朋友约翰和哈里特——同时也是他们的邻居——寻求帮助。

"约翰,你可以在周六早上给艾玛打一个电话叫她去海边吗?"海伍德先生在电话里问道。"等她离开家之后,哈里特会过来帮我们做蛋糕和布置气球。"

"没问题!"约翰激动地回答道。

生日那天,当艾玛回到家时,她惊讶又高兴地听到所有的家人和朋友一起大喊着"生日快乐!",还为她唱起了生日歌。

"现在是你许愿的时间了,我的孩子。"海伍德太太拿着一个巧克力蛋糕出现了,她在艾玛的额头上轻轻地吻了一下。

"首先,谢谢大家来到这里。"艾玛微笑着看向每一个人,"现在是我许愿的时间了。"

"我希望成为奥运冠军的梦想可以实现。"艾玛闭着眼睛,双手合十,在心里默念。然后,她吹灭了所有的蜡烛。

艾玛的父母和朋友们送给她很多可爱的礼物。整个下午,他们在一起愉快地享受美食,玩着游戏。

"今天真是太有趣了!这是我最棒的生日回忆。"艾玛在她的日记里写道。

Word list

blonde [blɒnd] *adj.* 金发的

always ['ɔːlweɪz] *adv.* 总是;每次都是
近义 all the time 一直

friendly ['frendli] *adj.* 友好的;亲切的

搭配 a friendly smile 亲切的微笑

other ['ʌðə(r)] *det. & pron.* 另外;其他
搭配 each other 互相,彼此

ago [ə'gəʊ] *adv.* 以前

搭配 days ago 几天前

become [bɪˈkʌm] v. 成为；变得；变成
搭配 become famous 成名；扬名

interested [ˈɪntrəstɪd] adj. 感兴趣的
例句 Bob is interested in maths. 鲍勃对数学很感兴趣。

afterwards [ˈɑːftəwədz] adv. 以后；后来

allow [əˈlaʊ] v. 允许
搭配 be allowed to do sth 被允许做某事

take [teɪk] v. 拿；获得；采取；买；耗费
搭配 take part in 参与，参加
take off 起飞；脱下

birthday [ˈbɜːθdeɪ] n. 生日，诞辰
搭配 a birthday party 生日派对
助记 birth（出生）+day（日）

decide [dɪˈsaɪd] v. 决定；下决心
例句 I can't decide what to wear. 我拿不定主意穿什么。

who [huː] pron.（询问姓名、身份或职务）谁
例句 Who are you? 你是谁？

teenager [ˈtiːneɪdʒə(r)] n.（13至19岁之间的）青少年
例句 She is still a teenager. 她依然是个青少年。

neighbour [ˈneɪbə(r)] n. 邻居
例句 Our neighbour is very kind. 我们的邻居非常友善。

give somebody a call 给某人打电话
同义 give somebody a ring 给某人打电话

after [ˈɑːftə(r)] adv. 后来，以后 prep. 在……之后
例句 They lived happily ever after. 从此以后他们过上了幸福的生活。

balloon [bəˈluːn] n. 气球

excited [ɪkˈsaɪtɪd] adj. 兴奋的；激动的；活跃的
搭配 excited kids 激动的孩子们

kid [kɪd] n. 小孩
注意 kid 一般用于口语；child 一般用于书面语。

kiss [kɪs] v. & n. 吻
例句 Mum gave me a kiss. 妈妈给了我一个吻。

look at 看
例句 Let's look at it again, shall we? 我们再看一遍，好不好？

lovely [ˈlʌvli] adj. 可爱的；令人愉快的
例句 Jessica is a lovely girl. 杰西卡是个可爱的女孩。

gift [ɡɪft] n. 礼物；天赋
同义 present 礼物

together [təˈɡeðə(r)] adv. 一起；同时
例句 We grew up together. 我们是在一起长大的。

happily [ˈhæpɪli] adv. 快乐地；高兴地

whole [həʊl] adj. 完整的 n. 整体；全部
搭配 as a whole 总体上

interesting [ˈɪntrəstɪŋ] adj. 有趣的；引起兴趣的
例句 He is an interesting guy. 他是一个有趣的人。

memory [ˈmeməri] n. 记忆，记忆力；回忆（pl. memories）
搭配 good memories 美好的记忆

Exercise

Ⅰ. Listen and read the phrases and sentences aloud.

1. take part in a competition
2. birthday party and birthday gift
3. Happy birthday!
4. lovely and friendly
5. What an interesting day!
6. best memory
7. give somebody a call
8. neighbours and friends

Ⅱ. Label the pictures.

1. k_ _   2. f_ _ _ _ _ _ _   3. k_ _ _

4. g_ _ _   5. b_ _ _ _ _ _   6. n_ _ _ _ _ _ _ _

7. b_ _ _ _ _ _   8. l_ _ _ _ _   9. t_ _ _ _ _ _ _   10. m_ _ _ _ _

Ⅲ. Listen and fill in the blanks. Write one word or a number for each blank.

Emma's Birthday Party Plan

When: next Saturday

Where: at Mr and Mrs Haywood's house

Number of guests: 1. _____

Preparation: a chocolate cake, flowers, candles, and 2. _____

Mr Haywood's gift: a 3. _____ about sailing

Ⅳ. Read the email from your pen-friend, Andy.

From:	Andy
To:	

Hello! It's nice to know you. My name is Andy and I'm ten years old. I live in New York. What about you? How many people are there in your family? Do you have good friends?

Write an email to Andy and answer the questions.

Write **25 words** or more.

_____

_____

_____

_____

Unit 2
House and Home

Pre-test

快速浏览下面的单词，自测一下，看看你是否已经掌握了呢？记得标记你不熟悉的单词，多多复习哦！

- ☐ roof [ruːf] n. 屋顶
- ☐ lorry [ˈlɒri] n. 卡车
- ☐ sink [sɪŋk] n.（厨房里的）洗碗槽
- ☐ brush [brʌʃ] n. 刷子；毛刷
- ☐ cycle [ˈsaɪkl] n. 自行车；摩托车
- ☐ channel [ˈtʃænl] n. 电视台
- ☐ housewife [ˈhaʊswaɪf] n. 主妇；家庭妇女
- ☐ seem [siːm] v. 好像，似乎
- ☐ stage [steɪdʒ] n. 阶段；舞台
- ☐ then [ðen] adv. 那时；然后
- ☐ wake [weɪk] v. 醒来
- ☐ wake up 醒来
- ☐ rent [rent] v. 租用；出租
- ☐ quarter [ˈkwɔːtə(r)] n.（正点之前或之后的）15分钟，一刻钟
- ☐ what [wɒt] det. & pron. 什么
- ☐ a. m. [ˌeɪ ˈem] adv. 上午
- ☐ p. m. [ˌpiː ˈem] adv. 下午
- ☐ pet [pet] n. 宠物
- ☐ cat [kæt] n. 猫
- ☐ dog [dɒɡ] n. 狗
- ☐ exit [ˈeksɪt] n. 出口
- ☐ million [ˈmɪljən] num. 百万
- ☐ pull [pʊl] v. 拉
- ☐ push [pʊʃ] v. 推
- ☐ another [əˈnʌðə(r)] det. & pron. 另一（事物或人）
- ☐ mirror [ˈmɪrə(r)] n. 镜子

故事导读：
1. 小朋友，你知道怎样用英语来描述自己的家吗？来看看Evan是怎样介绍他的家的吧。
2. 如果遇到不熟悉的单词，记得标记出来哦。

Evan's Home Tour (1)

Welcome! My name is Evan, and I'm your homestay host. I would love to show you around my house today. I live here with my wife Luna, my daughter Mia, and my son James.

Now we're at the gate. You can see the garden, where we plant many flowers. The garage is on your left. That's also the place we keep large rubbish bins.

Open the door and walk in, and we're now standing at the front hall. On the ground floor, there's a large living room. My wife likes these floor-to-ceiling windows because they can make more natural light get in. The sitting area has a cosy sofa, a couple of chairs, and a soft carpet. Mia and James usually sit on the carpet to read.

Luna and I decided to put a bookcase instead of a television in our living room because we believe that reading is better for our kids than watching TV. We have various reading time every week and you're welcome to join. In winter, when the temperature(温度) outside is low, it is very lovely to enjoy a book beside the fireplace.

The kitchen is certainly my favourite place in the house. I love cooking. We have various cooking tools and equipment. The oven and the fridge are a little bit old, but they're still working well. Plates and cups are in these drawers and cupboards. We don't use the dining room very often. Only when we have guests do we use it.

参观埃文的家（一）

参考译文

欢迎你！我叫埃文，我是你的寄宿家庭的主人。今天我非常乐意带你参观一下我的房子。我和我的妻子卢娜、女儿米娅，还有儿子詹姆斯一起住在这里。

现在我们在大门口，你可以看到我们在花园里种了许多花。你的左手边是车库，那里也是我们存放大垃圾桶的地方。

打开门往里走，我们现在站在前厅里。一楼有一个很大的客厅。我的妻子非常喜欢这些落地窗，因为它们能让更多的自然光照射进来。休息区域有一张舒适的沙发、几把椅子，还有一张柔软的地毯。米娅和詹姆斯经常坐在地毯上看书。

卢娜和我决定在客厅里放一个书架，而不是电视，因为我们相信：对孩子们来说，阅读比看电视更好。我们每周都有家庭阅读时间，我们也非常欢迎你加入我们。在冬天，当外面的温度很低的时候，坐在壁炉旁边看书真的是再幸福不过了。

厨房绝对是我在家里最喜欢的地方了。我很喜欢做饭。我们有各种各样的烹饪工具和设备。烤箱和冰箱有点儿旧了，但是依然很好用。盘子和杯子放在这些抽屉和橱柜里。我们并不经常使用餐厅，只在客人到访的时候才会用到。

Word list

home [həʊm] *n.* 家，住宅；家乡
搭配 stay at home 待在家里

house [haʊs] *n.* 房屋；住宅
搭配 a two-bedroom house 两居室的住宅

today [tə'deɪ] *n. & adv.* 今天，今日

live [lɪv] *v.* 居住；生存；生活
例句 She needs to find somewhere to live. 她需要找个住的地方。

gate [geɪt] *n.* 大门；出入口
搭配 the gate of the city 城门

garden ['gɑːdn] *n.* 花园；菜园
搭配 a rose garden 玫瑰花园

garage ['gærɑːʒ] *n.* 停车房；车库
搭配 a bus garage 公共汽车车库

rubbish ['rʌbɪʃ] *n.* 垃圾，废物

bin [bɪn] *n.* 垃圾箱；箱子，容器
搭配 a rubbish bin 垃圾箱

door [dɔː(r)] *n.* 门
搭配 open the door 开门

stand [stænd] *v.* 站立；位于
搭配 stand up 起立

hall [hɔːl] *n.* 过道；门厅
例句 She ran into the hall and up the stairs. 她跑进门厅，冲上楼梯。

floor [flɔː(r)] *n.* 地板；楼层
例句 I live on the ground floor. 我住在一楼。

there [ðeə(r)] *adv.* 表示存在；在那里

living room 客厅；起居室
同义 sitting room 客厅，起居室

ceiling ['siːlɪŋ] *n.* 天花板

搭配 a large room with a high ceiling 天花板很高的大房间

light [laɪt] *n.* 光；光线；灯
搭配 a room with good natural light 采光好的房间

area [ˈeərɪə] *n.* 地区；区域
搭配 a picnic area 野餐区

sofa [ˈsəʊfə] *n.* 沙发；长椅

chair [tʃeə(r)] *n.* 椅子
搭配 a table and chairs 一套桌椅

carpet [ˈkɑːpɪt] *n.* 地毯；地毯状覆盖物
搭配 a roll of carpet 一卷地毯

sit [sɪt] *v.* 坐；位于
例句 May I sit here? 我可以坐在这儿吗？

bookcase [ˈbʊkkeɪs] *n.* [家具] 书柜，书架
助记 book（书）+case（容器）

television [ˈtelɪvɪʒn] *n.* 电视（缩写 TV）

believe [bɪˈliːv] *v.* 相信；认为
例句 I don't believe you! 我不相信你的话！

watch [wɒtʃ] *v.* 观看，注视；看守
搭配 watch TV 看电视

time [taɪm] *n.* 时间；时代
例句 What time is it? 几点了？

low [ləʊ] *adj.* 低的；浅的
例句 The temperature is too low. 温度太低了。

book [bʊk] *n.* 书

kitchen [ˈkɪtʃɪn] *n.* 厨房
搭配 in the kitchen 在厨房里

certainly [ˈsɜːtnli] *adv.* 肯定；当然，行（用于回答）
例句 I'm certainly never going there again. 我肯定不会再去那里了。

equipment [ɪˈkwɪpmənt] *n.* 设备；装备
搭配 office equipment 办公室设备

oven [ˈʌvn] *n.* 烤箱；炉，灶
例句 Take the cake out of the oven. 把蛋糕从烤箱中取出来。

fridge [frɪdʒ] *n.* 电冰箱
例句 There's nothing much in the fridge. 冰箱里没什么东西了。

drawer [drɔː(r)] *n.* 抽屉
搭配 open the desk drawer 打开书桌抽屉

cupboard [ˈkʌbəd] *n.* 橱柜；衣柜
搭配 kitchen cupboards 厨房里用的橱柜

dining room 餐厅

Exercise

I. Listen and read the phrases aloud.

1. the house with a garden and a garage
2. rubbish bin
3. stand at the front hall
4. living room and dining room
5. floor and ceiling
6. sofa and chair
7. reading and watching television
8. drawer and cupboard
9. oven and fridge
10. cooking tools and equipment

II. Label the pictures.

  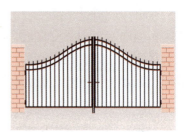

1. g _ _ _ _ _   2. g _ _ _ _ _   3. g _ _ _

4. r _ _ _ _ _ _ b _ _

5. l _ _ _ _ _ _ r _ _ _   10. c _ _ _ _
6. s _ _ _   11. o _ _ _
7. c _ _ _ _ _   12. f _ _ _ _ _
8. b _ _ _ _ _ _ _   13. c _ _ _ _ _ _ _
9. t _ _ _ _ _ _ _ _ _   14. d _ _ _ _ _

III. Listen and choose the correct answer for each question.

1. Where is the boy's English textbook?

   A. On the bookcase.

   B. On the sofa.

   C. In his bag.

2. How many plates do they need for the dinner?

   A. 8.   B. 6.   C. 2.

3. Where did Jack have dinner yesterday?

   A. In the kitchen.

   B. In the dining room.

   C. In the living room.

IV. Answer the questions.

1. How many rooms are there in your home? What are they?

   _____

   _____

2. Where do you watch TV?

   _____

   _____

3. Where do you and your family have dinner?

   _____

   _____

故事导读：
1. 小朋友，让我们继续听Evan介绍他的家吧。
2. 如果有不熟悉的单词，记得标记出来哦。

Evan's Home Tour (2)

Now let's walk up the stairs. There're three bedrooms and two bathrooms on the first floor. The largest room is the master bedroom. The colours of the wooden furniture and the curtains are matched. My wife has lots of clothes, so I made her a walk-in closet.

Next is James' bedroom. There's a single bed, a cabinet, a shelf, a desk and an armchair in his room. He wants to keep it simple. Mia lives in the opposite room. Sometimes her friends stay overnight and sleep in her room.

Your room is on the second floor. We painted your walls with a bright colour. Have you noticed flowers beside the lamp and the alarm clock? Mia picked them from the garden. We hope you like them.

We got new pillows and bed sheets for you. If you feel cold at night, you can find a blanket in the wardrobe. The heating system is powered by electricity, and you can adjust the temperature on your own. The toilet is on the right side. You can take a shower, but if you want to use the bathtub, you need to go downstairs. We have also prepared shampoo and towels. By the way, Luna will help you tidy up your room and your toilet every week. Please don't make these places too dirty.

It's five o'clock now and I'm afraid that I have got to leave for a while. Here is your key. We'll have dinner in one and a half hours.

参观埃文的家（二）

现在我们上楼吧。二楼有三间卧室和两个卫生间。最大的这个房间是主卧。木家具和窗帘的颜色是搭配的。我的妻子有很多衣服，所以我给她做了一个步入式衣帽间。

接下来是詹姆斯的卧室。他的房间里有一张单人床、一个橱柜、一个架子、一张桌子和一把扶手椅。他希望自己的房间简单就好。米娅的房间在对面。有时候她的朋友会来过夜，睡在她的房间里。

你的房间在三楼。我们给你房间的墙刷上了明亮的颜色。你注意到台灯和闹钟旁边的花了吗？那是米娅在花园里采的。我们希望你能喜欢。

我们为你准备了新枕头和床单。如果你晚上觉得冷，可以在衣柜里找到毯子。供暖系统是电热的，你可以自己调节温度。厕所在你的右手边。你可以淋浴，但是如果你需要用浴缸，就得下楼了。我们还给你准备了洗发水和毛巾。顺便说一下，卢娜每周都会帮你清理房间和厕所。希望你不要把它们弄得特别脏。

现在已经五点了，我恐怕不得不离开一会儿。这是你的钥匙。我们会在一个半小时后吃晚餐。

Word list

stair [steə(r)] n. 楼梯
例句 The children ran up the stairs. 孩子们跑上楼梯。

bedroom [ˈbedruːm] n. 卧室
搭配 the master bedroom 主卧
助记 bed（床）+ room（房间）

bathroom [ˈbɑːθruːm] n. 浴室；厕所；盥洗室
助记 bath（洗澡）+ room（房间）

wooden [ˈwʊdn] adj. 木制的
搭配 a wooden box 木箱

furniture [ˈfɜːnɪtʃə(r)] n. 家具
搭配 a piece of furniture 一件家具

curtain [ˈkɜːtn] n. 窗帘
搭配 close the curtains 拉上窗帘

closet [ˈklɒzɪt] n. 贮藏室；壁橱
搭配 a walk-in closet 步入式衣帽间

single [ˈsɪŋɡl] adj. 单一的；单身的
搭配 a single bed 单人床

bed [bed] n. 床
例句 It's time for bed. 该是睡觉的时候了。

cabinet [ˈkæbɪnət] n. 储藏柜；陈列柜
搭配 a medicine cabinet 药柜

shelf [ʃelf] n. 架子；搁板
搭配 a shoe shelf 鞋架

armchair [ˈɑːmtʃeə(r)] n. 扶手椅
搭配 sit in an armchair 坐在扶手椅上

simple [ˈsɪmpl] adj. 简单的
搭配 a simple solution 简单的解决办法

stay [steɪ] v. 停留；暂住
搭配 stay in bed 待在床上；卧病在床

sleep [sliːp] v. 睡，睡觉（过去式/过去分词 slept）
例句 I had to sleep on the sofa. 我只得睡在沙发上。

wall [wɔːl] n. 墙壁；围墙

lamp [læmp] n. 灯
搭配 a desk lamp 台灯

clock [klɒk] n. 时钟
搭配 an alarm clock 闹钟

pillow [ˈpɪləʊ] n. 枕头

sheet [ʃiːt] n. 床单

blanket [ˈblæŋkɪt] n. 毛毯，毯子

wardrobe [ˈwɔːdrəʊb] n. 衣柜；衣橱
搭配 a new wardrobe 一个新衣柜

heating [ˈhiːtɪŋ] n. 供暖
搭配 a gas heating system 燃气供暖系统

electricity [ɪˌlekˈtrɪsəti] n. 电
例句 The electricity is off. 停电了。

own [əʊn] adj. 自己的；特有的
搭配 on one's own 独自；独立地
例句 I need a room of my own. 我需要一个独立的房间。

toilet [ˈtɔɪlət] n. 厕所；马桶
搭配 public toilets 公共厕所

shower [ˈʃaʊə(r)] n. 淋浴；淋浴间
搭配 take a shower 淋浴

bathtub [ˈbɑːθtʌb] n. 浴缸

助记 bath（洗澡）+ tub（浴盆）

shampoo [ʃæmˈpuː] n. 洗发液
搭配 a bottle of shampoo 一瓶洗发液

towel [ˈtaʊəl] n. 毛巾，手巾
搭配 a bath towel 浴巾

tidy [ˈtaɪdi] v. 整理；收拾 adj. 整洁的；整齐的
例句 You should tidy up before leaving. 你出去之前一定要收拾一下。

dirty [ˈdɜːti] adj. 肮脏的；卑鄙的
例句 Try not to get too dirty! 别把身上弄得太脏！

o'clock [əˈklɒk] adv. ……点钟
例句 He left between five and six o'clock. 他是五六点钟离开的。

have got to 必须；不得不
例句 We have got to leave right now. 我们必须马上离开。

key [kiː] n. 钥匙 adj. 关键的
搭配 the door key 门钥匙

half [hɑːf] n. 一半 det. & pron. 半数
搭配 one and a half hours 一个半小时
half an hour 半小时

hour [ˈaʊə(r)] n. 小时
例句 He'll be back in an hour. 他一小时后回来。

Exercise

1. Listen and read the phrases and sentence aloud.

   1. bedroom and bathroom
   2. wooden furniture and curtain

3. closet, cabinet and wardrobe
4. shower and bathtub
5. shampoo and towel
6. pillow and sheet
7. bed and armchair
8. single and simple
9. tidy up my room
10. I have got to leave.

II. Label the pictures.

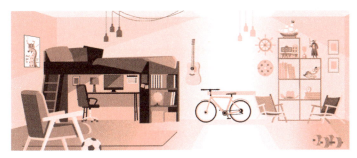

1. b _ _ _ _ _ _   2. b _ _   3. p _ _ _ _ _
4. s _ _ _ _   5. b _ _ _ _ _ _   6. l _ _ _
7. s _ _ _ _   8. c _ _ _ _   9. a _ _ _ _ _ _ _

10. b _ _ _ _ _ _ _   11. t _ _ _ _ _
12. s _ _ _ _ _   13. b _ _ _ _ _ _
14. s _ _ _ _ _ _   15. t _ _ _ _

III. Listen and choose the correct answer for each question. 🔊

1. Which is Ivan's room?

A

B

2. Where do Mr Smith and his family read books together every week?

A

B

3. How will William take a bath today?

A

B

IV. **Look at the three pictures.**

Write the story shown in the pictures.

Write **35 words** or more.

_____

_____

_____

_____

Unit 3
Education

Pre-test

快速浏览下面的单词，自测一下，看看你是否已经掌握了呢？记得标记你不熟悉的单词，多多复习哦！

- ☐ advanced [əd'vɑːnst] adj. 先进的
- ☐ note [nəʊt] n. 笔记
- ☐ teach [tiːtʃ] v. 训练
- ☐ diary ['daɪəri] n. 日记
- ☐ borrow ['bɒrəʊ] v. 借；借用
- ☐ broken ['brəʊkən] adj. 破损的
- ☐ copy ['kɒpi] v. 复制；作弊
- ☐ correct [kə'rekt] adj. 正确的
- ☐ give back 归还；恢复
- ☐ cover ['kʌvə(r)] v. 遮盖 n. 封皮
- ☐ lend [lend] v. 借给；借出
- ☐ national ['næʃnəl] adj. 国家的；民族的
- ☐ page [peɪdʒ] n. 页；张
- ☐ paragraph ['pærəgrɑːf] n. 段；段落
- ☐ degree [dɪ'griː] n. 程度；（大学）学位
- ☐ mine [maɪn] pron. 我的
- ☐ one [wʌn] det. & pron. 一
- ☐ per [pə(r)] prep. 每；每一
- ☐ ourselves [ˌaʊə'selvz] pron. 我们自己
- ☐ herself [hɜː'self] pron. 她自己
- ☐ itself [ɪt'self] pron. 它本身
- ☐ find [faɪnd] v. 发现

故事导读：
1. 小朋友，你还记得第一天上学的情形吗？来看看 Ethan 在新学校的第一天是怎样的吧。
2. 遇到不熟悉的单词要标记出来哦。

Ethan's First Day at the New School

Ethan is a fifth-grade pupil and today is his first day at the new school. He just moved to this country with his family. He is very nervous because he has to use a foreign language at school.

"Mum, what if I say something wrong in class? What if I get low marks and fail the exams?" asked Ethan anxiously the day before.

"Take it easy, my dear. No one will laugh at you," answered Ethan's mother kindly. "You're a clever boy. You have studied English for many years. What's more, do you know that making mistakes is the best way to learn a language? Just believe in yourself and don't be afraid."

"I can make it." Ethan whispered to himself before falling asleep.

Ethan got up early in the morning and went to the school with his parents. They met the headteacher, Mrs Thompson, at her office. She gave Ethan's parents a student guidebook and then took him to the classroom.

"Let's give a warm welcome to Ethan. He just moved here, so I hope everyone can help him fit in." Mrs Thompson wrote down Ethan's name on the blackboard.

"My name is Ethan and I'm from China. My favourite subjects are history and science. I like playing volleyball and reading books after school." Ethan introduced himself in the front of the class and then sat next to a boy with blond hair.

"Everyone is friendly and nice!" said Ethan to his parents at dinner time, "I can't wait to see my new classmates tomorrow!"

读故事 巧记 KET 核心词汇

伊森在新学校的第一天

伊森是一名五年级小学生，今天是他在新学校的第一天。他刚刚和他的家人一起搬到这个新的国家。由于他必须在学校里使用外语，所以他感到非常紧张。

"妈妈，假如我在课堂上说错了话怎么办？假如我的成绩特别差，考试通不过怎么办？"去上学的前一天，伊森焦虑地问道。

"放松点，亲爱的。没有人会笑话你的。"伊森的妈妈亲切地回答道。"你是一个聪明的男孩。你已经学习英语很多年了。另外，你知道吗？犯错误是学习一门语言的最好方式。你一定要相信自己，不要害怕。"

"我一定可以做到的。"伊森在睡觉之前悄悄地对自己说道。

清晨，伊森早早地起床了，和爸爸妈妈一起去学校。他们在办公室里见到了校长汤普森太太。她给了伊森的父母一份学生手册，然后带他去了教室。

"让我们热烈欢迎伊森。他刚刚搬到这里，我希望大家能够帮助他适应新环境。"汤普森太太在黑板上写下了伊森的名字。

"我叫伊森，我来自中国。我最喜欢的科目是历史和科学。放学后，我喜欢打排球和读书。"伊森在教室前面做了自我介绍，然后坐在了一个金发男孩旁边。

"每个人都很友好、很亲切！"伊森吃晚饭时对爸爸妈妈说道，"我迫不及待想明天再次见到我的新同学了！"

Word list

grade [greɪd] *n.* 年级；等级
例句 Sam is in the second grade. 萨姆读二年级。

pupil [ˈpjuːpl] *n.* 小学生
例句 How many pupils does the school have? 这所小学有多少学生？

school [skuːl] *n.* （中、小）学校
例句 School begins at 9. 学校9点开始上课。

this [ðɪs] *det. & pron.* 这，这个 (*pl.* these)
例句 Is this your bag? 这是你的包吗？

have to 必须；不得不
例句 Do you have to go? 你必须走吗？

foreign [ˈfɒrən] *adj.* 外国的
搭配 a foreign language 外语

language [ˈlæŋɡwɪdʒ] *n.* 语言
例句 Chinese is my first language. 汉语是我的母语。

wrong [rɒŋ] *adj.* 错误的
例句 I got all the answers wrong. 我的答案全错了。

class [klɑːs] *n.* 班级；课
例句 I was late for class. 我上课迟到了。

mark [mɑːk] *n.* 成绩；分数 *v.* 做标记
搭配 get a good mark in English 英语得高分

fail [feɪl] v. 失败；不及格
例句 He failed his driving test. 他没通过驾驶执照考试。

exam [ɪɡˈzæm] n. 考试
搭配 take an exam 参加考试
同义 examination 考试

easy [ˈiːzi] adj. 容易的
搭配 take it easy 放松点

no one 没有人
例句 No one was at home. 没有人在家。

answer [ˈɑːnsə(r)] v. & n. 答复；回答
搭配 answer the question 回答问题

clever [ˈklevə(r)] adj. 聪明的（比较级 cleverer；最高级 cleverest）
搭配 a clever child 聪明的孩子

study [ˈstʌdi] v. 学习
搭配 study English 学英语

know [nəʊ] v. 知道；了解（过去式 knew；过去分词 known）

mistake [mɪˈsteɪk] n. 错误
例句 Don't worry; we all make mistakes. 没关系，我们都会犯错。

learn [lɜːn] v. 学习；学会（过去式/过去分词 learnt 或 learned）
搭配 learn a language 学一门语言

yourself [jɔːˈself] pron. 你自己（pl. yourselves 你们自己）
例句 Help yourself! 请自便！/随便吃！

himself [hɪmˈself] pron. 他自己
例句 He introduced himself. 他做了自我介绍。

get up 起床
例句 I usually get up at six. 我通常六点钟起床。

early [ˈɜːli] adj. 早的 adv. 早（比较级 earlier；最高级 earliest）

headteacher [ˈhedtiːtʃə] n.（中小学）校长；班主任
助记 head（领头）+teacher（教师）

student [ˈstjuːdnt] n. 学生
搭配 a high school student 高中生

guidebook [ˈɡaɪdbʊk] n. 指南；手册
助记 guide（向导）+book（书）

classroom [ˈklɑːsruːm] n. 教室
搭配 in the classroom 在教室里

write [raɪt] v. 书写，写字（过去式 wrote；过去分词 written）
搭配 write down 写下

blackboard [ˈblækbɔːd] n. 黑板
助记 black（黑色的）+board（板子）

subject [ˈsʌbdʒekt] n. 主题；学科
例句 Biology is my favourite subject. 生物是我最喜爱的学科。

history [ˈhɪstri] n. 历史；历史学

science [ˈsaɪəns] n. 科学
搭配 science and technology 科学技术

read [riːd] v. 阅读
搭配 read the newspaper 看报纸

classmate [ˈklɑːsmeɪt] n. 同班同学
助记 class（班级）+mate（同伴）

Exercise

I. Listen and read the phrases and sentences aloud.

1. get up early and go to school
2. read a student guidebook
3. write down your answer on the blackboard
4. get low marks and fail the exams
5. You're a clever boy.
6. Take it easy and believe in yourself.
7. My favourite subjects are history and science.
8. Making mistakes is the best way to learn a foreign language.

II. Label the pictures.

1. s _ _ _ _ _

2. c _ _ _ _ _ _ _ _

3. b _ _ _ _ _ _ _ _ _

4. s _ _ _ _ _ _

5. g _ _   u _

6. m _ _ _ _ _ _

7. g _ _ _ _ _ _ _ _

8. m _ _ _

9. r _ _ _

10. w _ _ _ _

Day 5

III. Listen and choose the correct answer for each question.

1. Did Samantha fail the maths exam?
   A. Yes.　　　　　B. No.　　　　　C. Not given.
2. What is Karl's favourite subject?
   A. History.　　　B. English.　　　C. Science.
3. Who is Karl and Samantha's new PE teacher?
   A. Mr Johnson.　B. Mr McAvoy.　C. Mr Blair.

IV. Answer the questions.

1. Do you like going to school?

_____

_____

2. How many students are there in your class?

_____

_____

3. What is your favourite subject?

_____

_____

故事导读：
1. 小朋友，让我们一起听听 Thompson 校长是怎样介绍学校的吧。
2. 记得把不熟悉的单词标记出来哟。

An Introduction to the School

I'm Mrs Thompson and I'm the headteacher of this international primary school. Let me give you an introduction to our school.

Students usually get to school around 8:20 a.m. If they arrive after 8:30 a.m., they will be marked late. Before the morning lessons, teachers give various tasks to those schoolchildren to get ready for the day. These tasks could be finished by themselves or in pairs.

During the courses of the day, students will take part in all the subjects: reading, writing, maths, science, and social studies. The class timetable is written on the board. In the blocks of Language Arts, students are given reading instructions about the articles in their textbooks, as well as practice in spelling, handwriting and vocabulary. In the maths class, teachers give a mini-lesson and then students have 40 minutes of group or independent work. The last 10 minutes is used to summarise what was learnt and prepare for further learning. Science classes include the content of beginner level biology, geography, physics and chemistry. Students need to pass all the final tests to get their diplomas.

At the beginning of a new school term, we invite alumni（校友）of different nationalities who graduated from top colleges and universities to give lectures. We hope that students can better find out their interests and explore their future.

The school day usually ends around 3 p.m. Before going back home, children often finish the jobs like cleaning the desks, putting paper materials and dictionaries back to the bookshelf, putting pencils, pens, rulers and rubbers in the schoolbags. In the end, homework is given out and recorded in every student's notebook.

学校简介

我是汤普森太太，这所国际小学的校长。让我来给你介绍一下我们学校吧。

学生们通常在早上 8:20 左右到达学校。如果他们 8:30 以后到校，就会被记为迟到。上午的课程开始之前，老师会给学生们布置各种各样的任务，来帮助他们为这一天的学习做好准备。这些任务都是由学生们独自完成或者结伴完成的。

在一天的课程中，学生们会参与所有科目：阅读、写作、数学、科学和社会研究。白板上写着课程表。在语言艺术课程中，老师会指导学生阅读课文，学生也会进行有关拼写、书法和词汇的练习。在数学课上，老师会先开展迷你教学，然后学生们会进行 40 分钟的小组学习或者独立学习。最后 10 分钟用于总结已经学习过的知识，并为学习新知识做准备。科学课内容包含初级水平的生物、地理、物理和化学知识。学生们必须通过所有的期末考试才能拿到毕业证书。

新的学期一开始，我们会邀请来自不同国家、毕业于顶尖学院和大学的校友们发表演讲。我们希望学生们可以更好地发现自己的兴趣所在并探索自己的未来。

学校的一天通常会在下午 3 点左右结束。在回家之前，孩子们经常要完成下列工作，比如清理桌子、把纸质材料和字典放回书架，还要把铅笔、钢笔、尺子和橡皮等放进书包。最后，老师会布置家庭作业，每个学生会在笔记本上记录下来。

international [ˌɪntəˈnæʃnəl] *adj.* 国际的
搭配 international students 国际学生

late [leɪt] *adj.* 迟到的；晚的
例句 I'm sorry I'm late. 对不起，我迟到了。

lesson [ˈlesn] *n.* 课
例句 What did we learn last lesson? 我们上节课学了什么内容？

those [ðəʊz] *det. & pron.* 那些（that 的复数形式）

schoolchild [ˈskuːltʃaɪld] *n.* 学童；小学生
（*pl.* schoolchildren）
助记 school（学校）+ child（儿童）

these [ðiːz] *det. & pron.* 这些（this 的复数形式）

finish [ˈfɪnɪʃ] *v.* 完成；结束
例句 Did you finish your homework? 你完成家庭作业了吗？

themselves [ðəmˈselvz] *pron.* 他们自己；他们亲自
例句 They've bought themselves a new car.

他们给自己买了一辆新车。

pair [peə(r)] *n.* 一对，一双
搭配 work in pairs 两人一组练习

maths [mæθs] *n.* 数学（英式）
全称 mathematics 数学
同义 math 数学（美式）

studies [ˈstʌdiz] *n.* 研究；学业（study 的复数形式）
搭配 social studies 社会研究

board [bɔːd] *n.* 木板

instruction [ɪnˈstrʌkʃn] *n.* 用法说明；指导
搭配 reading instructions 阅读指导

article [ˈɑːtɪkl] *n.* 文章
搭配 write an article 写文章

textbook [ˈtekstbʊk] *n.* 教科书，课本
搭配 a history textbook 历史教科书
助记 text（文本）+book（书）

practice [ˈpræktɪs] *n.* 练习
搭配 conversation practice 会话练习

vocabulary [vəˈkæbjələri] *n.* 词汇；词汇量
近义 word 单词

last [lɑːst] *adj.* 最后的

further [ˈfɜːðə(r)] *adj.* 更多的；更进一步的
搭配 further reading 延伸阅读

beginner [bɪˈɡɪnə(r)] *n.* 初学者；新手
例句 She's in the beginners' class. 她在初级班。

level [ˈlevl] *n.* 水平；级别
搭配 language level 语言水平

biology [baɪˈɒlədʒi] *n.* 生物学

geography [dʒiˈɒɡrəfi] *n.* 地理学
搭配 social geography 社会地理学

physics [ˈfɪzɪks] *n.* 物理学

chemistry [ˈkemɪstri] *n.* 化学

pass [pɑːs] *v.* 通过；传递
例句 She hasn't passed her driving test yet. 她还没有通过驾驶执照考试。

final [ˈfaɪnl] *adj.* 最终的
搭配 make the final decision 做出最后的决定

test [test] *n.* 测试，考查
搭配 take a test 参加测试

diploma [dɪˈpləʊmə] *n.* 毕业文凭
搭配 a high school diploma 高中毕业文凭

term [tɜːm] *n.* 学期
搭配 the spring/summer/autumn term 春季/夏季/秋季学期

nationality [ˌnæʃəˈnæləti] *n.* 国籍
搭配 have French nationality 拥有法国国籍

college [ˈkɒlɪdʒ] *n.* （英国）学院；（美国）大学
例句 She's at college. 她在学院读书。

university [ˌjuːnɪˈvɜːsəti] *n.* 大学
搭配 a university course 大学课程

find out 找出，查明；发现
搭配 find out the answer 找到答案

explore [ɪkˈsplɔː(r)] *v.* 探索
搭配 explore the old city 探索老城

future [ˈfjuːtʃə(r)] *n.* 未来
搭配 in the future 在将来

desk [desk] *n.* 书桌

paper [ˈpeɪpə(r)] *n.* 纸
搭配 a piece of paper 一张纸

dictionary [ˈdɪkʃənri] *n.* 字典；词典
搭配 a Chinese-English dictionary 汉英词典

bookshelf [ˈbʊkʃelf] *n.* 书架（*pl.* bookshelves）
助记 book（书）+shelf（架子）

pencil [ˈpensl] *n.* 铅笔

pen [pen] *n.* 钢笔

Day 6

ruler [ˈruːlə(r)] *n.* 尺子

rubber [ˈrʌbə(r)] *n.* 橡皮（英式）
同义 eraser 橡皮（美式）

homework [ˈhəʊmwɜːk] *n.* 家庭作业

notebook [ˈnəʊtbʊk] *n.* 笔记本
助记 note（笔记）+ book（书）

Exercise

I. Listen and read the phrases aloud.

1. pen, pencil, ruler and rubber
2. find out and explore
3. notebook and textbook
4. college and university
5. maths, physics, chemistry, biology and geography
6. a dictionary on the bookshelf
7. pass the final tests to get diplomas
8. finish homework by themselves or in pairs

II. Match the pictures with the words.

Group 1

1.   A. textbook
2.   B. ruler
3.   C. pencil
4.   D. pen
5.   E. rubber

Group 2

1.   A. bookshelf
2.   B. desk
3.   C. dictionary
4.   D. paper
5.   E. notebook

Ⅲ. **Listen and choose the correct answer for each question.**

1. Who has borrowed Ann's maths textbook?
   A. Christina.   B. Mike.   C. Not given.
2. Who should clean the desks today?
   A. Danny.   B. Bobby.   C. Jane.
3. What time did Ben arrive at school today?
   A. At 8:15 a.m.   B. At 8:20 a.m. C. At 8:35 a.m.

Ⅳ. **Read the email from your English pen-friend, Ethan.**

From:	Ethan
To:	

Hello! My name is Ethan and I'm a fifth-grade pupil. History and science are my favourite subjects. I bring my pencil case and notebooks to school every day. Which grade are you in? What subjects are you good at? What do you bring to school every day?

Write an email to Ethan and answer his questions.

Write **25 words** or more.

_____

_____

_____

_____

Unit 4
Shopping and Clothes

Pre-test

快速浏览下面的单词，自测一下，看看你是否已经掌握了呢？记得标记你不熟悉的单词，多多复习哦！

- ☐ bag [bæg] n. 袋子；手提包
- ☐ tights [taɪts] n. （女用）连裤袜，紧身裤
- ☐ cap [kæp] n. 软扁帽；制服帽
- ☐ jeans [dʒiːnz] n. (pl.) 牛仔裤
- ☐ suit [suːt] n. 套装；西装
- ☐ dress [dres] n. 连衣裙 v. 穿衣服
- ☐ get dressed 穿上衣服
- ☐ sweater ['swetə(r)] n. 毛衣
- ☐ pocket ['pɒkɪt] n. 口袋
- ☐ good-looking [ˌɡʊd 'lʊkɪŋ] adj. 漂亮的；好看的
- ☐ least [liːst] adv. 最小；最少
- ☐ at least 至少
- ☐ normal ['nɔːml] adj. 正常的；一般的
- ☐ scissors ['sɪzəz] n. (pl.) 剪刀
- ☐ bill [bɪl] n. 账单
- ☐ cost [kɒst] v. & n. 花费
- ☐ cent [sent] n. 分
- ☐ dollar ['dɒlə(r)] n. 元（美国、加拿大、澳大利亚以及其他一些国家的货币单位）
- ☐ price [praɪs] n. 价格
- ☐ cheap [tʃiːp] adj. 便宜的；廉价的
- ☐ euro ['jʊərəʊ] n. 欧元
- ☐ advert ['ædvɜːt] n. 广告
- ☐ shut [ʃʌt] v. 关闭

故事导读：
1. 小朋友，你喜欢和好朋友一起去买衣服吗？来看看Vivien和Olivia的购物经历吧。
2. 记得把不熟悉的单词标记一下哦。

Let's Go Shopping for Clothes!

Vivien and Olivia are good friends and they usually go shopping together.

"Hi! This is Viv. Have you read the advertisement for the Central Shopping Centre? There are many clothes on sale. I need a new jacket or a new coat, as well as a new pair of boots. Would you like to come?" asked Vivien on the phone.

"I've read that! There are so many discounts. I also want to buy new clothes, maybe a nice T-shirt or a blouse. By the way, the jumper I bought last time doesn't fit me well so I need to change the size. Let's meet around three," answered Olivia.

They met at the entrance of the shopping centre. "Look at the poster over there! The model in the striped shirt and slim trousers looks great. We should go to that store and have a look," said Vivien with excitement.

"Good afternoon! Is there anything I can help?" A shop assistant gave Vivien and Olivia a polite greeting when they walked in.

"Yes. I'd like to try on what the model wears on that poster." Vivien requested while looking around the shop.

"Certainly. If you're interested, I also recommend you try on this A-line skirt with black and white stripes and that pair of shorts. They both match perfectly with that shirt." The shop assistant suggested with a smile.

"Why not?" Vivien tried them on and decided to take them all.

"500 pounds? It's a bit expensive, isn't it?" Olivia whispered to Vivien when she checked out.

"They're all **half-price**!" Vivien said, "I need the clothes and I want to **spend** my **money** on them."

我们一起去买衣服吧！

薇薇安和奥利维亚是好朋友，她们经常一起去购物。

"嗨！我是小薇。你看到中央购物中心的广告了吗？很多衣服都在打折。我需要一件新夹克或者新外套，还有一双新靴子。你想和我一起去吗？"薇薇安在电话里问道。

"我看到了！很多商品在打折。我也想买新衣服，比如一件漂亮的T恤或者女士衬衣。对了，我上次买的套头毛衣不太合身，所以我得去换一个尺码。我们三点左右见面吧。"奥利维亚回答道。

她们俩在购物中心的入口处见了面。"你看那边的海报！那个穿着条纹衬衣和瘦腿裤的模特看起来太棒了。我们应该去那家店里看看。"薇薇安兴奋地说道。

"下午好，请问需要什么帮助吗？"一名店员在薇薇安和奥利维亚走进店时礼貌地问候了她们。

"嗯，我想试穿一下那张海报上模特穿的衣服。"薇薇安一边环顾商店，一边回应道。

"没问题。如果您感兴趣的话，我推荐您也试穿一下这条带有黑白条纹的A字裙，还有那条短裤。它们都和那件衬衣特别搭。"店员面带微笑地给出了建议。

"为什么不试试呢？"薇薇安全都试穿了一遍，决定全都买下。

"500英镑？有点贵，是不是？"奥利维亚在薇薇安结账时小声说道。

"已经是半价了！"薇薇安说，"我需要这些衣服，所以我愿意花钱买下它们。"

Word list

shopping [ˈʃɒpɪŋ] n. 购物
搭配 go shopping 去购物

advertisement [ədˈvɜːtɪsmənt] n. 广告（简称 ad）

clothes [kləʊðz] n. 衣服
搭配 take off one's clothes 脱下衣服

sale [seɪl] n. 销售；出售
搭配 for sale 出售；待售

on sale 廉价出售

jacket [ˈdʒækɪt] n. 短上衣；夹克衫
搭配 a leather jacket 皮夹克

coat [kəʊt] n. 外套；大衣

boot [buːt] n. 靴子
搭配 a pair of black leather boots 一双黑皮靴

discount [ˈdɪskaʊnt] n. 折扣 v. 对……打折
搭配 at a discount 打折

give a discount 给予折扣

buy [baɪ] *v.* 买；购买（过去式/过去分词 bought）

T-shirt ['tiːʃɜːt] *n.* T恤衫
搭配 a printed T-shirt 印花T恤衫

blouse [blaʊz] *n.* 女式衬衫
搭配 a sleeveless blouse 无袖衬衫

jumper ['dʒʌmpə(r)] *n.* （毛或棉的）针织套衫，毛衣（英式）
同义 sweater 毛衣（美式）

change [tʃeɪndʒ] *v. & n.* 改变；更换
例句 We'll change it for a larger size. 我们会给您换件大号的。

size [saɪz] *n.* 大小；尺码
例句 It's not my size. 这个尺码不适合我。

poster ['pəʊstə(r)] *n.* 海报，广告
搭配 put up a poster 张贴海报

model ['mɒdl] *n.* 模特；模型
搭配 a fashion model 时装模特

striped [straɪpt] *adj.* 有条纹的；有斑纹的
搭配 a striped shirt 一件条纹衬衫

shirt [ʃɜːt] *n.* （尤指男士）衬衫
搭配 wear a shirt and tie 穿衬衫，扎领带

slim [slɪm] *adj.* 苗条的；纤细的
例句 She is tall and slim. 她是瘦高个儿。

trousers ['traʊzəz] *n.* 裤子（英式）
搭配 a pair of grey trousers 一条灰裤子
同义 pants 裤子（美式）

should [ʃəd] *mv.* 应该
例句 What should I do? 我应该做些什么？

store [stɔː(r)] *n.* 商店
搭配 a food store 食品店

shop [ʃɒp] *n.* 商店；店铺
搭配 a shoe shop 鞋店

assistant [ə'sɪstənt] *n.* 助手，助理
搭配 a shop assistant 店员；售货员

polite [pə'laɪt] *adj.* 有礼貌的
搭配 polite requests 礼貌的请求

try [traɪ] *v.* 尝试
搭配 try on 试穿

wear [weə(r)] *v.* 穿；戴
例句 She always wears black clothes. 她总是穿黑色的衣服。

line [laɪn] *n.* 线；线条
搭配 a straight line 直线

skirt [skɜːt] *n.* 裙子
搭配 a long/short skirt 长/短裙

stripe [straɪp] *n.* 条纹
搭配 black and white stripes 黑白条纹

shorts [ʃɔːts] *n.* 短裤
搭配 He was wearing a T-shirt and shorts. 他那时穿着T恤衫和短裤。

pound [paʊnd] *n.* 英镑

expensive [ɪk'spensɪv] *adj.* 昂贵的；花钱多的
例句 That dress is expensive. 那条连衣裙很贵。

half-price [ˌhɑːf 'praɪs] *adj.* 半价的
搭配 a half-price ticket 半价票

spend [spend] *v.* 用，花（钱）（过去式/过去分词 spent）
例句 She spent £100 on a new dress. 她花100英镑买了一条新连衣裙。

money ['mʌni] *n.* 钱
搭配 spend money 花钱

Exercise

I. Listen and read the phrases aloud.

1. go shopping for clothes
2. polite shop assistant and good-looking model
3. on sale and discount
4. advertisement and poster
5. try on a new pair of boots
6. jumper and sweater
7. shirt and blouse
8. jacket and coat
9. a pair of shorts and slim trousers
10. striped dress and A-line skirt with stripes
11. dollar, pound and euro
12. spend money on something

II. Label the pictures.

1. T-_____

2. b_____

3. s_____

4. t_____

5. b____

6. j_____

7. s____

8. j_____

9. c___

10. m____

Ⅲ. Listen and choose the correct answer for each question. 🔊

1. Who bought Jack a T-shirt yesterday?

   A   B

2. What will Daisy wear to school?

   A   B

3. Which is Jacob?

   A   B

Ⅳ. Answer the questions.

1. Do you like going shopping for clothes?

_____

_____

2. Who do you usually go shopping with?

_____

_____

3. What are you wearing now?

_____

_____

故事导读：
1. 小朋友，学完这篇文章之后，试着描述一下你常去的那家商场吧。
2. 遇到不熟悉的单词记得标记出来哦。

Welcome to the Central Shopping Centre

Dear customers, welcome to the Central Shopping Centre. We open at 11 a.m. and close at 9 p.m. from Monday to Sunday.

We sell many products, including clothing, jewellery and accessories(配饰), housewares(厨房用具), food and drinks, and much more.

The jewellery and accessory section is on the ground floor. We sell all types of jewellery, including rings, bracelets, necklaces, earrings which are made of gold, silver and gems. Accessories are next to jewellery, including leather handbags, purses and wallets, watches, sunglasses, ties and belts. There's also a wide choice of hats, scarfs and gloves. The make-up and perfume counters are also on the same floor, where you can buy all sorts of items.

The clothing stores and shoe stores are on the first floor. The products we sell include clothing and shoes in the latest fashion for women, men and children. You can also find sportswear, sports socks, swimming costumes, and sporting equipment on this floor.

On the second floor, there are many restaurant chains. There's also a large market where you can buy fresh food.

Customers can pay by credit card, cheque or in cash at any store. After checkout, please keep your receipts which can be used for a refund. We provide umbrellas and raincoats for shoppers to borrow on rainy days. If you have any questions, please feel free to ask our staff for help. They wear blue uniforms.

We always put "customers first" and "make sure every penny you spend counts". Thank you for choosing us and we sincerely hope to see you soon!

欢迎光临中央购物中心

亲爱的顾客，欢迎光临中央购物中心。我们每周一到周日上午11点开门，晚上9点关门。

我们售卖多种商品，有服饰、珠宝及配饰、厨房用具、食物饮料，等等。

珠宝及配饰专区位于一楼。我们售卖各种类型的首饰，包括金、银和宝石制成的戒指、手镯、项链和耳环。首饰旁边就是配饰，包括皮包、男女钱包、手表、太阳镜、领带和皮带。这里还有各种各样的帽子、围巾和手套可供选择。化妆品和香水柜台也在这一层，您可以购买各种各样的化妆品。

服装店和鞋店位于二楼。我们销售的产品包括最新款的男女服装、童装和男女鞋、童鞋。您还可以在这一层找到运动服饰、运动袜、泳装和各种运动器材。

三楼有很多餐厅连锁店，还有一家大型市场，在那里您可以买到新鲜的食物。

顾客可以使用信用卡、支票或者现金在任意一家商店内付款。结账后，请保存好收据，以便退款。下雨天，我们会向顾客出借雨伞和雨衣。如果您有任何疑问，请尽管向工作人员寻求帮助。他们穿着蓝色制服。

我们一直把"顾客至上"放在第一位，并"确保您花的每一分钱都是值得的"。非常感谢您选择我们，我们诚挚地希望您能够再次光临！

Word list

customer [ˈkʌstəmə(r)] *n.* 顾客
搭配 customer first 顾客至上

welcome [ˈwelkəm] *exclam.* 欢迎 *adj.* 受欢迎的
例句 Welcome home! 欢迎回家！

open [ˈəʊpən] *v.* 打开 *adj.* 开着的
搭配 open the window 打开窗户

close [kləʊz] *v.* 关闭（closed *adj.* 关闭的）
搭配 close the window 关上窗户

sell [sel] *v.* 售卖（过去式/过去分词 sold）

jewellery [ˈdʒuːəlri] *n.* 珠宝（英式）
搭配 silver jewellery 银首饰
同义 jewelry 珠宝（美式）

type [taɪp] *n.* 类型；种类
例句 I love this type of book. 我喜欢这类图书。

ring [rɪŋ] *n.* 戒指
搭配 a gold ring 金戒指

bracelet [ˈbreɪslət] *n.* 手镯；手链
搭配 a silver bracelet 银手镯

necklace [ˈnekləs] *n.* 项链

助记 neck（脖子）+ lace（花边）

earring [ˈɪərɪŋ] *n.* 耳环，耳饰
搭配 a pair of earrings 一对耳环

gold [gəʊld] *n.* 黄金 *adj.* 金色的

leather [ˈleðə(r)] *n.* 皮革
搭配 a leather belt 皮带

handbag [ˈhændbæg] *n.* 小手提包
助记 hand（手）+ bag（包）

purse [pɜːs] *n.* （女士）钱包
例句 I took a coin out of my purse. 我从钱包里取出了一枚硬币。

wallet [ˈwɒlɪt] *n.* 钱包，皮夹

sunglasses [ˈsʌnˌɡlɑːsɪz] *n.* 太阳镜
助记 sun（太阳）+ glasses（眼镜）

tie [taɪ] *n.* 领带
搭配 a striped silk tie 带有条纹的真丝领带

belt [belt] *n.* 腰带；皮带
搭配 seat belt 安全带

hat [hæt] *n.* 帽子
搭配 put on a hat 戴帽子

scarf [skɑːf] *n.* 围巾
搭配 a silk scarf 丝绸围巾

glove [glʌv] *n.* 手套
搭配 a pair of gloves 一副手套

make-up [ˈmeɪk ʌp] *n.* 化妆品
搭配 wear make-up 化妆

perfume [ˈpɜːfjuːm] *n.* 香水
搭配 a bottle of expensive perfume 一瓶昂贵的香水

sort [sɔːt] *n.* 种类；方式
例句 What sort of music do you like? 你喜欢哪一类音乐？

shoe [ʃuː] *n.* 鞋

搭配 a pair of shoes 一双鞋

latest [ˈleɪtɪst] *adj.* 最新的；最近的
搭配 the latest style 最新款式

fashion [ˈfæʃn] *n.* 时尚；流行款式
搭配 out of fashion 过时

sock [sɒk] *n.* 短袜
搭配 a pair of socks 一双短袜

costume [ˈkɒstjuːm] *n.* （特定国家或历史时期流行的）服装；全套服饰
搭配 swimming costume 泳衣（英式）
＝ bathing suit（美式）

chain [tʃeɪn] *n.* 连锁；链子
搭配 a supermarket chain 连锁超市

market [ˈmɑːkɪt] *n.* 市场
搭配 a fruit market 水果市场

pay [peɪ] *v.* 支付
搭配 pay for 支付

credit card 信用卡
例句 Are you paying in cash or by credit card? 您付现金还是刷信用卡？

cheque [tʃek] *n.* 支票（英式）
搭配 pay by cheque 用支票支付
同义 check 支票（美式）

cash [kæʃ] *n.* 现金

receipt [rɪˈsiːt] *n.* 收据；收条

umbrella [ʌmˈbrelə] *n.* 雨伞

raincoat [ˈreɪnkəʊt] *n.* 雨衣
助记 rain（雨）+ coat（外套）

shopper [ˈʃɒpə(r)] *n.* 购物者；顾客

free [friː] *adj.* 自由的；免费的
例句 Feel free to ask questions if you don't understand. 你要是不懂，可以随便提问。

uniform [ˈjuːnɪfɔːm] *n.* 制服

penny [ˈpeni] *n.* 便士 (*pl.* pennies 或 pence)

例句 He has a few pennies in his pocket. 他的口袋里有几便士。

thank [θæŋk] *v.* 谢谢，感谢

例句 Thank you (= Thanks) very much. 非常感谢你。

soon [suːn] *adv.* 很快；马上；不久

例句 See you soon! 再见！

Exercise

Ⅰ. Listen and read the phrases aloud.

1. open and close
2. sell and buy
3. necklace and bracelet
4. ring and earring
5. purse and wallet
6. tie and belt
7. glove and scarf
8. make-up and perfume
9. umbrella and raincoat
10. credit card and cash

Ⅱ. Match the pictures with the words.

Group 1

1.   A. socks
2.   B. umbrella
3.   C. handbag
4.   D. sunglasses
5.   E. raincoat

Group 2

1.   A. bracelet
2.   B. ring
3.   C. wallet
4.   D. uniform
5.   E. necklace

III. **For each question, write the correct answer in the gap. Write one word or one number.**

Capital Mall

Date: 24th September
Closing Time: 1. _____ p. m.
Which floor has clothing: 2. The _____ floor
Not pay by: 3. _____

IV. **Look at the three pictures.**

Write the story shown in the pictures.
Write **35 words** or more.

_____

_____

_____

_____

Unit 5
Food and Drink

Pre-test

快速浏览下面的单词，自测一下，看看你是否已经掌握了呢？记得标记你不熟悉的单词，多多复习哦！

- ☐ cola ['kəʊlə] n. 可乐饮料
- ☐ cooker ['kʊkə(r)] n. 厨灶，炉具
- ☐ salt [sɔːlt] n. 盐
- ☐ curry ['kʌri] n. 咖喱
- ☐ cut [kʌt] v. 切；割
- ☐ box [bɒks] n. 盒；箱
- ☐ melon ['melən] n. 甜瓜
- ☐ cafeteria [ˌkæfə'tɪəriə] n. 自助餐厅；自助食堂
- ☐ add [æd] v. 增加
- ☐ oil [ɔɪl] n. 石油；原油
- ☐ candy ['kændi] n. 糖果（美式）
- ☐ else [els] adv. 其他
- ☐ fat [fæt] adj. 肥胖的 n. 肥肉
- ☐ many ['meni] det. & pron. 许多
- ☐ picnic ['pɪknɪk] n. 野餐
- ☐ wash [wɒʃ] v. 洗
- ☐ little ['lɪtl] adj. 小的
- ☐ bit [bɪt] n. 少量 adv. 有点儿；稍微
- ☐ mix [mɪks] v. （使）混合，掺和

故事导读：
1. 你对美食感兴趣吗？来看看 Aria 家的派对上都有什么美食吧。
2. 记得把不熟悉的单词标记出来哦。

Aria's Daily Vlog（1）

Hey guys, this is Aria! Welcome back to my channel! Today is my husband Tommy's birthday and we'll have a small dinner party at our house. Follow me and see how it goes!

Now we're in the backyard. The weather is nice and we're going to eat outside. We set the table earlier in the morning. We got these beautiful bowls, plates and cups from abroad, and this set of silverware, which includes knives, forks and spoons, is a gift from a friend. We only take them out for special days, like today.

We invited several friends a few weeks ago. They were told to bring one of their favourite desserts, which means we're going to have some really delicious home-made sweet snacks! Patrick, Emily and Anne will bring some banana cakes, mango rice, butter biscuits and fruit sugars. I love their desserts so much and I never have enough.

Look, who is in the kitchen? Tommy's mum just finished baking a lovely birthday cake and now is preparing for tonight's barbecue. As you see, the bottom of the cake is decorated with lots of cream, and on the top, there're some strawberry slices and chocolate bars. We hope Tommy will like it.

Now I'm going to pick some apples and lemons from our backyard. It would be great to make some fresh drinks like juice, lemonade, cocktails and fruit tea with them to serve our thirsty guests.

It's already three o'clock and I have to start preparing for the cooking. See you later!

阿丽亚的视频日记（一）

嗨，大家好！我是阿丽亚。欢迎回到我的频道！今天是我丈夫汤米的生日，我们会在家里举办一次小型的聚餐。跟我来看看进展如何吧！

现在我们在后院。今天天气很好，我们会在室外用餐。我们今天一大早就布置好了餐桌。我们有从国外买来的漂亮的碗、碟和杯子，以及朋友送的一套镀银餐具，包括刀、叉和勺子。我们通常只在特殊的日子里使用它们，比如今天。

几周前我们就邀请了几位朋友。我们告诉他们要带一样自己最爱的甜品，这意味着我们将会吃到一些非常美味的自制甜点心！帕特里克、艾米丽和安妮会带香蕉蛋糕、芒果饭、黄油饼干以及水果糖。我特别喜欢他们的甜品，感觉永远都吃不够。

来看看是谁在厨房里？汤米的妈妈刚烤完一个漂亮的生日蛋糕，现在正在为晚上的烧烤做准备。你看，蛋糕的底部有大量的奶油裱花，顶部则有一些草莓块和巧克力棒。我们希望汤米会喜欢这个蛋糕。

现在我要去后院采摘一些苹果和柠檬。我会用它们制作一些新鲜的饮品，比如果汁、柠檬水、鸡尾酒以及水果茶，用来招待我们口渴的客人。

现在已经三点了，我得开始为烹饪做准备了。一会儿见！

Word list

dinner [ˈdɪnə(r)] n. 晚餐，晚宴
搭配 Christmas dinner 圣诞大餐

how [haʊ] adv. 如何；怎样
例句 How are you? 你（身体）好吗？

eat [iːt] v. 吃；吃饭（过去式 ate；过去分词 eaten）
例句 I don't eat meat. 我不吃肉。

table [ˈteɪbl] n. 桌子；表格
搭配 set the table 摆饭桌

bowl [bəʊl] n. 碗

plate [pleɪt] n. 盘子；碟子
搭配 a pile of dinner plates 一叠餐盘

cup [kʌp] n. 杯子
搭配 a coffee cup 咖啡杯

set [set] n. 一套 v. 放，置；摆放餐具
搭配 a set of six chairs 六把成套的椅子

knife [naɪf] n. 刀（pl. knives）
搭配 a bread knife 切面包刀

fork [fɔːk] n. 餐叉
搭配 eat with a knife and fork 用刀叉吃东西

spoon [spuːn] n. 匙；勺子
搭配 a soup spoon 汤匙

several [ˈsevrəl] det. & pron. 几个；数个
搭配 several times 几次

a few 一些；几个
搭配 a few months ago 几个月之前

favourite [ˈfeɪvərɪt] adj. 特别喜爱的 n. 特别喜爱的人（或事物）
例句 Who is your favourite writer? 谁是你特别喜欢的作家？

dessert [dɪˈzɜːt] n.（饭后）甜点，甜食
例句 What's for dessert? 餐后甜点吃什么？

delicious [dɪˈlɪʃəs] adj. 美味的；可口的
搭配 delicious dessert 美味的甜品

sweet [swiːt] adj. 甜的 n. 糖果（英式）
搭配 sweet food 甜食
同义 candy 糖果（美式）

snack [snæk] n. 小吃；快餐
搭配 snack food 零食

banana [bəˈnɑːnə] n. 香蕉
搭配 a bunch of bananas 一串香蕉

cake [keɪk] n. 蛋糕
搭配 a piece of cake 一块蛋糕

mango [ˈmæŋɡəʊ] n. 芒果
搭配 a fresh mango 新鲜的芒果

rice [raɪs] n. 大米；米饭
搭配 a bowl of rice 一碗米饭

butter [ˈbʌtə(r)] n. 黄油，奶油
例句 Much of our butter comes from New Zealand. 我们的很多黄油产自新西兰。

biscuit [ˈbɪskɪt] n. 饼干
搭配 chocolate biscuits 巧克力饼干

sugar [ˈʃʊɡə(r)] n. 糖
搭配 fruit sugars 水果糖

enough [ɪˈnʌf] det. 足够的 pron. 足够的人或事物 adv. 足够
例句 Have you had enough? 你吃饱了吗？

bake [beɪk] v. 烤，烘焙
例句 I'm baking Alex a cake. 我在给亚历克斯烤蛋糕。

barbecue [ˈbɑːbɪkjuː] n. 户外烤肉
例句 Let's have a barbecue! 我们来一次户外烧烤吧！

bottom [ˈbɒtəm] n. 底部
搭配 at the bottom of the hill 在山脚下

lots of 许多；大量
搭配 lots of sugar 大量的糖
同义 a lot of 许多；大量

cream [kriːm] n. 奶油，乳脂
搭配 fresh cream 新鲜的奶油

strawberry [ˈstrɔːbəri] n. 草莓
搭配 strawberry ice cream 草莓冰激凌

slice [slaɪs] n. 薄片
搭配 a slice of bread 一片面包

chocolate [ˈtʃɒklət] n. 巧克力
搭配 a chocolate cake 巧克力蛋糕

apple [ˈæpl] n. 苹果
例句 I want an apple. 我想要一个苹果。

lemon [ˈlemən] n. 柠檬

fresh [freʃ] adj. 新鲜的；清新的
搭配 vegetables fresh from the garden 刚从菜园采摘的蔬菜

drink [drɪŋk] n. 饮料 v. 喝，饮（过去式 drank；过去分词 drunk）
例句 Can I have a drink? 给我来一杯饮料好吗？
I don't drink coffee. 我不喝咖啡。

juice [dʒuːs] n. 果汁
搭配 fresh apple juice 新鲜的苹果汁

lemonade [ˌleməˈneɪd] n. 柠檬水
例句 When life gives you lemon, make

lemonade. 当生活给你柠檬的时候，把它做成柠檬汁吧。

tea [tiː] *n.* 茶
例句 Do you take sugar in your tea? 你的茶里放糖吗？

thirsty [ˈθɜːsti] *adj.* 口渴的
例句 We are hungry and thirsty. 我们又饥又渴。

cooking [ˈkʊkɪŋ] *n.* 烹饪；饭菜
例句 They serve good French cooking. 他们供应美味的法国菜。

Exercise

I. Listen and read the phrases aloud.

1. fresh drinks and delicious desserts
2. bowl, cup and plate
3. knife, fork and spoon
4. apple and banana
5. mango and strawberry
6. lemon and lemonade
7. butter and cream
8. set the table and have dinner
9. bake a chocolate cake
10. have a barbecue

II. Label the pictures.

1. c _ _ _

2. a _ _ _ _

3. b _ _ _ _ _

4. m _ _ _ _

5. s _ _ _ _ _ _ _ _ _

6. l _ _ _ _

7. t _ _ _ _

8. b _ _ _

9. p _ _ _ _   10. s _ _ _ _
11. f _ _ _   12. c _ _

III. Listen and choose the correct answer for each question.

1. What is Jack's favourite fruit?
   A. The apple.　　　B. The banana.　　　C. The orange.
2. What is the food that Josh will bring to Tom's birthday party?
   A. A strawberry cake.　B. Chocolate biscuits.　C. Cream cupcakes.
3. What do you think the man is going to have?
   A. Orange juice.　　B. Tea.　　　　　　C. Coffee.

IV. Answer the questions.

1. What fruit do you usually eat?

   _____

   _____

2. What do you usually have for dinner?

   _____

   _____

3. What do you usually use to have dinner?

   _____

   _____

故事导读：
1. 小朋友，你喜欢去餐厅吃饭吗？让我们继续跟着Aria的镜头，来了解更多美食吧。
2. 如果有不熟悉的单词，记得标记一下哦。

Aria's Daily Vlog (2)

Hi, this is Aria! Welcome back to my channel! It's lunchtime now; Tommy and I are on the way to a restaurant on an empty stomach. We thought that we would order some fast food like pizza or burger because we were really hungry, but we eventually decided to have some healthy food.

Now we are sitting at a restaurant. The waiter just brought us two glasses of mineral water and the lunch menu. For starters (前菜), we decide to try their famous fish soup and egg salad. For main courses, I would like to have a steak which goes with chips and fried mushrooms while Tommy wants a Sunday roast.

Have you heard of Sunday roast? Here it is. As you see, it's a traditional British main meal. It is usually served with roast meat and boiled potatoes. You can choose from chicken, lamb, pork or beef along with different kinds of sauces. Vegetables such as carrots, beans and broccoli (西兰花) can also be part of the dish. Yum, it tastes really good!

It's already half past two and we just bought two cups of coffee at our favourite cafe. I think we have eaten too much and we are too full now. We decide to have a walk and drop by the supermarket to get some stuff for tonight's supper and tomorrow's breakfast.

We finally get back home! We get some bread and sausages to make sandwiches, some jam, and a large bottle of milk.

Thank you for watching! Please leave a comment below and wish to see you soon!

阿丽亚的视频日记（二）

参考译文

嗨，我是阿丽亚。欢迎回到我的频道。现在是午餐时间了，汤米和我正饿着肚子走在去餐厅的路上。因为我们太饿了，本来考虑点一些快餐，比如比萨饼或者汉堡，但最终还是决定去吃一些健康的食物。

现在我们已经坐在餐厅里了。服务员刚给我们拿来两杯矿泉水和午餐菜单。至于前菜，我们决定尝试一下这家餐厅著名的鱼汤和鸡蛋沙拉。至于主菜，我决定点一份搭配薯条和煎蘑菇的牛排，而汤米决定点一份周日烤肉。

你听说过周日烤肉吗？就是它。如你所见，这是一份传统的英式主菜，通常有烤肉和水煮土豆。你可以选择鸡肉、羊肉、猪肉或者牛肉，并搭配各种各样的酱汁。胡萝卜、青豆和西兰花等蔬菜也是这道菜的一部分。真好吃，尝起来真不错！

已经两点半了，我们刚在我们最爱的咖啡馆买了两杯咖啡。我觉得我们吃得太多了，现在肚子太撑了。我们决定去散步，顺路去超市买一些今天晚餐和明天早餐的食材。

我们终于到家了！我们买了一些用来做三明治的面包和香肠，一些果酱，还有一大瓶牛奶。

谢谢你们的观看！请在下方留下评论，希望可以很快再次见到你们！

Word list

lunchtime [ˈlʌntʃtaɪm] n. 午餐时间
助记 lunch（午餐）+time（时间）
搭配 during lunchtime 在午餐时间

empty [ˈempti] adj. 空的
搭配 fill an empty stomach 填饱肚子

order [ˈɔːdə(r)] v. 点 n. 点菜
例句 I ordered a beer and a sandwich. 我点了一杯啤酒和一份三明治。

fast food 速食，快餐
搭配 a fast food shop 快餐店

pizza [ˈpiːtsə] n. 比萨饼

burger [ˈbɜːgə(r)] n. 汉堡包

hungry [ˈhʌŋgri] adj. 饥饿的
例句 I'm really hungry. 我确实饿了。

food [fuːd] n. 食物

搭配 food and drink 饮食

waiter [ˈweɪtə(r)] n. 服务员
联想 waitress n. 女服务员

water [ˈwɔːtə(r)] n. 水
搭配 mineral water 矿泉水

lunch [lʌntʃ] n. 午餐
例句 What shall we have for lunch? 我们午餐吃什么？

menu [ˈmenjuː] n. 菜单
搭配 look at the menu 看菜单

fish [fɪʃ] n. 鱼；鱼肉
注意 fish 指"鱼的条数"时，单数和复数形式都是 fish，比如：two fish 两条鱼；fish 指"鱼的种类"时，复数形式是 fishes，比如：two fishes 两种鱼；fish 指"鱼肉"时，是不可数名词。

soup [suːp] n. 汤
搭配 a bowl of soup 一碗汤

egg [eg] n. 蛋；鸡蛋
搭配 a boiled egg 煮鸡蛋

salad [ˈsæləd] n. 沙拉
搭配 fruit salad 水果沙拉

main course 主菜；主要课程
例句 After the main course, would you like some dessert? 吃完主菜后，您想来点甜点吗？

steak [steɪk] n. 牛排；肉排
搭配 pork steak 猪排
例句 How would you like your steak done? 您的牛排煎到几成熟？

chip [tʃɪp] n. 炸薯条（英式）
搭配 fish and chips 炸鱼薯条
同义 French fries 炸薯条（美式）

mushroom [ˈmʌʃrum] n. 蘑菇
搭配 cream of mushroom soup 奶油蘑菇汤

roast [rəʊst] n. 烤肉 adj.（食物）烤过的 v. 烘，烤（肉等）
搭配 roast chicken 烧鸡
roast a chicken 烤一只鸡

meal [miːl] n. 一顿饭；（一顿所吃的）食物
例句 Enjoy your meal. 请用餐。

serve [sɜːv] v. 提供，供应
例句 Breakfast is served between 7 and 10 a.m. 早餐供应时间是7点到10点。

meat [miːt] n.（供食用的）肉
搭配 a piece of meat 一块肉

boil [bɔɪl] v. 煮沸；用沸水煮（过去式/过去分词 boiled）
搭配 boiled potatoes 水煮土豆

potato [pəˈteɪtəʊ] n. 土豆；马铃薯（pl. potatoes）
搭配 roast potatoes 烤土豆

sauce [sɔːs] n. 酱；调味汁
搭配 tomato sauce 番茄酱

bean [biːn] n. 豆

dish [dɪʃ] n. 盘；（一道）菜
搭配 a cold dish 凉菜

coffee [ˈkɒfi] n. 咖啡
例句 Would you like some coffee? 你想喝点咖啡吗？

cafe [ˈkæfeɪ] n. 咖啡馆；小餐馆

much [mʌtʃ] adv. 非常，很 det. & pron. 大量，多少（比较级 more；最高级 most）
例句 You worry too much. 你过于担心了。
How much is it? 这东西多少钱？

full [fʊl] adj. 满的，充满的
搭配 be full of 充满……
例句 No more for me, thanks—I'm full up. 谢谢，我不要了——我已经饱了。

stuff [stʌf] n. 东西
例句 Where's all my stuff? 我的那些东西在哪儿？

supper [ˈsʌpə(r)] n. 晚餐；晚饭
例句 We'll have an early supper tonight. 今天我们要早点吃晚饭。

breakfast [ˈbrekfəst] n. 早餐；早饭
例句 What's for breakfast? 早餐吃什么？

bread [bred] n. 面包
搭配 bread and butter 面包和黄油

sausage [ˈsɒsɪdʒ] n. 香肠
搭配 beef/pork sausages 牛肉/猪肉香肠

sandwich [ˈsænwɪtʃ] n. 三明治（pl. sandwiches）

搭配 a cheese sandwich 奶酪三明治

jam [dʒæm] n. 果酱

搭配 strawberry jam 草莓酱

bottle ['bɒtl] n. 瓶子；一瓶（的量）

搭配 a water bottle 水瓶
　　　a bottle of water 一瓶水

milk [mɪlk] n. 牛奶

搭配 a bottle of milk 一瓶牛奶

Exercise

Ⅰ. Listen and read the phrases aloud.

1. breakfast, lunch and supper
2. pizza and burger
3. soup and salad
4. fish and chips
5. bread and sandwich
6. roast meat and potatoes
7. hungry and thirsty
8. waiter and waitress
9. steak and sausage
10. water and coffee

Ⅱ. Match the pictures with the words.

Group 1

1. ____   A. fish
2. ____   B. steak
3. ____   C. coffee
4. ____   D. sandwich
5. ____   E. bread

Group 2

1. ____   A. mushroom
2. ____   B. salad
3. ____   C. sausage
4. ____   D. soup
5. ____   E. potato

III. Listen and then match the people and the food they order.

People	Food
1. Charles ☐	A. a beef sandwich
2. Andrew ☐	B. mushroom soup with bread
3. Susan ☐	C. a burger with chips
	D. a sausage pizza

IV. Read the email from your English pen-friend, Juno.

From:	Juno
To:	

Hello! My name is Juno and I live in the United Kingdom. My favourite food is the sausage pizza. We have roast meat dinner every Sunday.

What is your favourite food? What do you usually have for dinner on weekends? Who cooks in your family?

Write an email to Juno and answer the questions.

Write **25 words** or more.

_____

_____

_____

_____

Unit 6
Sport

Pre-test

快速浏览下面的单词，自测一下，看看你是否已经掌握了呢？记得标记你不熟悉的单词，多多复习哦！

- ☐ runner　　　　[ˈrʌnə(r)] n. 跑步者
- ☐ sea　　　　　[siː] n. 海；海洋
- ☐ luck　　　　　[lʌk] n. 好运，幸运
- ☐ bike　　　　　[baɪk] n. 自行车
- ☐ throw　　　　[θrəʊ] v. 投；扔
- ☐ catch　　　　 [kætʃ] v. 抓住；接住
- ☐ pool　　　　　[puːl] n. 游泳池；水池
- ☐ club　　　　　[klʌb] n. 俱乐部；社团
- ☐ versus　　　　[ˈvɜːsəs] prep. 对抗（缩写：V；VS）
- ☐ surf　　　　　[sɜːf] v. 冲浪
- ☐ cycling　　　　[ˈsaɪklɪŋ] n. 骑自行车运动
- ☐ fishing　　　　[ˈfɪʃɪŋ] n. 钓鱼
- ☐ riding　　　　[ˈraɪdɪŋ] n. 骑马
- ☐ extra　　　　　[ˈekstrə] adj. 额外的；附加的
- ☐ may　　　　　[meɪ] mv. 也许，可能
- ☐ surfing　　　　[ˈsɜːfɪŋ] n. 冲浪运动
- ☐ zero　　　　　[ˈzɪərəʊ] n. 零
- ☐ slow　　　　　[sləʊ] adj. 缓慢的
- ☐ slowly　　　　[ˈsləʊli] adv. 缓慢地
- ☐ go　　　　　　[gəʊ] v. 去；走
- ☐ point　　　　　[pɔɪnt] n. 得分 v. 指向

故事导读：
1. 小朋友，你去过现场观看体育比赛吗？和你的好朋友说说自己的感受吧。
2. 试着标出文中与运动项目相关的单词吧。

A Football Match

Kenny likes water sports, such as swimming, surfboarding, diving and windsurfing. He is also a big fan of football. In his opinion, football is more fantastic. Today he and his mum were watching a football match in the Olympic Stadium. Football players wearing special trainers were running from one side to the other.

"Mum, I really want to be a footballer so that I can kick the ball well, just like them," Kenny said to his mum.

"It's nice that you have a dream, but how much do you know about this sport?" asked Mum.

"In the UK, people call it football, but it's called soccer in America. American football is another sport like rugby," answered Kenny proudly.

"You are right, my boy. In fact, maybe it will take many years to be a famous player. You need to practise every day with your coach to enter a competition," Mum explained to Kenny.

"It seems not easy to be a footballer," said Kenny worriedly. Just then his favourite team scored one goal and their scores were much higher than those of the other team. They were about to win. "Yeah!" Kenny cried excitedly and jumped off the seat.

"This group is excellent and the players are strong. No matter which match they are in, they will be the winner."

"Of course," answered Kenny confidently.

(…)

"Kenny, look. I can't believe it — the group is about to lose. If they are a little faster, they will be the winner."

"That's not fair!" said Kenny sadly.

Mum told him gently, "Maybe they're just not lucky this time… We should believe they will get back and be the winner in the next event."

"Of course, they will," said Kenny.

一场足球赛

参考译文

肯尼喜欢水上运动，比如游泳、冲浪、潜水和风帆冲浪。同时他还是一个足球迷。在他看来，足球更美妙。今天，他和妈妈在奥林匹克体育场观看一场足球比赛。穿着专业运动鞋的足球运动员从一边跑到另一边。

"妈妈，我真的想成为一名足球运动员，这样我就能踢得像他们一样好。"肯尼对妈妈说。

"你有梦想是很棒的，但你对这项运动了解多少呢？"妈妈问道。

"在英国，人们叫它 football，但在美国，它被叫作 soccer。美式足球是另外一项运动，比较像橄榄球。"肯尼骄傲地答道。

"你说得对，我的孩子。事实上，成为一名著名的球员可能需要很多年。为了参加比赛，你需要每天和教练一起练习。"妈妈向肯尼解释道。

"看来做一名足球运动员似乎没那么容易。"肯尼担心地说。就在这时，他最喜欢的球队进了一球，而且他们的得分比另一队高出了很多，他们马上就要赢了。"耶！"肯尼兴奋地大喊着，从座位上跳了下来。

"这个团队非常优秀而且队员都很强壮。无论他们参加哪场比赛，他们都会是胜利者。"

"当然。"肯尼自信地回答道。

（……）

"肯尼，你看，简直不敢相信，这支球队居然要输了。如果他们再快一点的话，他们就赢了。"

"这不公平！"肯尼伤心地说。

妈妈温和地告诉他："可能是他们这次的运气不好……我们应该相信他们会重新上阵，取得下一场比赛的胜利。"

"当然，他们一定会的，"肯尼回答道。

Day 11

Word list

swimming [ˈswɪmɪŋ] n. 游泳
搭配 swimming pool 游泳池
联想 swim v. 游泳

surfboarding [ˈsɜːfbɔːdɪŋ] n. 冲浪运动
联想 surfboard n. 冲浪板

diving [ˈdaɪvɪŋ] n. 跳水；潜水
联想 dive v. 潜水

windsurfing [ˈwɪndsɜːfɪŋ] n. 帆板运动
联想 windsurf v. 风帆冲浪

fan [fæn] n. 迷；狂热爱好者

football [ˈfʊtbɔːl] n. 足球运动；橄榄球运动

fantastic [fænˈtæstɪk] adj. 精彩的；极好的
例句 The weather is absolutely fantastic. 天气非常好。

match [mætʃ] n. 比赛；火柴

Olympic [əˈlɪmpɪk] adj. 奥林匹克运动会的
搭配 the Olympic Games 奥运会

player [ˈpleɪə(r)] n. 运动员；游戏者

trainer [ˈtreɪnə(r)] n. 运动鞋（英式）
搭配 a pair of trainers 一双运动鞋
同义 sneaker 运动鞋（美式）

run [rʌn] v. 奔跑（过去式 ran；过去分词 run；现在分词 running）

kick [kɪk] v. 踢

ball [bɔːl] n. 球
搭配 kick the ball 踢球

sport [spɔːt] n. 运动

soccer [ˈsɒkə(r)] n. 足球运动

rugby [ˈrʌgbi] n. 橄榄球运动

fact [fækt] n. 事实；现实
搭配 in fact 事实上

maybe [ˈmeɪbi] adv. 大概，也许
注意 maybe 是副词，常用于句首，比如：Maybe she is in love. 也许她恋爱了。may be 是情态动词，may 加上 be 动词原形属于谓语，意为"可能是"，比如：He may be a teacher. 他可能是一位老师。

famous [ˈfeɪməs] adj. 著名的
例句 One day, I'll be rich and famous. 总有一天我会名利双收。

practise [ˈpræktɪs] v. 练习
例句 You need to practise every day. 你需要每天练习。

coach [kəutʃ] n. 教练；长途客车

enter [ˈentə(r)] v. 进入；报名参加
例句 Knock before you enter. 进来前请先敲门。

competition [ˌkɒmpəˈtɪʃn] n. 竞争；比赛
搭配 enter a competition 参加比赛

team [tiːm] n. （游戏或运动的）队
搭配 team work 团队合作

goal [gəʊl] n. 目标；进球
搭配 score a goal 进一球；得一分

high [haɪ] adj. 高的（比较级 higher；最高级 highest）

win [wɪn] v. 赢，获胜（过去式/过去分词 won）
例句 Which team won? 哪个队赢了？

jump [dʒʌmp] v. 跳

off [ɒf] *adv.* 离开，脱掉
搭配 jump off 跳下来

group [gruːp] *n.* 组；群；团体
搭配 a group of girls 一群女孩

excellent [ˈeksələnt] *adj.* 优秀的；极好的
例句 She speaks excellent French. 她的法语说得好极了。

strong [strɒŋ] *adj.* 强大的，强壮的（比较级 stronger；最高级 strongest）

matter [ˈmætə(r)] *n.* 事情；问题 *v.* 要紧
搭配 no matter what/how/who 无论是什么/如何/是谁
例句 It doesn't matter. 没关系。

winner [ˈwɪnə(r)] *n.* 获胜者

lose [luːz] *v.* 丧失，迷失，失败（过去式/过去分词 lost）
例句 He has lost his job. 他失业了。

fast [fɑːst] *adj.* 快速的（比较级 faster；最高级 fastest）

fair [feə(r)] *adj.* 公平的

lucky [ˈlʌki] *adj.* 幸运的
搭配 lucky dog 幸运儿

get back 恢复；回来

next [nekst] *adj.* 下一个的；紧接着的
搭配 next to 挨着，紧邻

event [ɪˈvent] *n.* 事件；比赛项目
例句 The main events start at 1 p.m. 主要项目下午1点开始。

Exercise

1. Listen and read these phrases aloud.

1. kick the ball and score a goal
2. run from one side to the other
3. jump off the boat and dive into the deep sea
4. watch a football match in the Olympic Stadium
5. surfboarding and windsurfing
6. player and coach
7. fantastic, excellent and well-known
8. enter a competition
9. lose and win
10. higher, faster and stronger

II. Match the words with the pictures.

Group 1

1. A. swimming
2. B. football
3. C. surfboarding
4. D. rugby
5. E. windsurfing

Group 2

1. A. kick
2. B. run
3. C. dive
4. D. jump
5. E. win

III. Listen and choose the correct answer for each question.

1. Which team was the winner?
   A. French team.　　　B. Canadian team.　　　C. Spanish team.
2. With whom will Anna watch the diving match?
   A. Her mum.　　　B. Her brother.　　　C. Her classmate.
3. Where are the speakers?
   A. On the beach.　　　B. In the swimming pool.　　　C. On the playground.

IV. Answer the questions.

1. What's your favourite sport and why?

_____

_____

2. Have you ever been a fan of a player?
   _____
   _____

3. When was Beijing Olympic Games held?
   _____
   _____

Day 12

故事导读：
1. 小朋友，试着找找 Tony 和 Stacy 最喜欢的运动分别是什么吧。
2. 试着圈出自己最喜欢的运动项目吧。

Two Sports Fans

Tony was having a rest in the sports centre when he met Stacy.

"Stacy, you skate so well! Are you good at skateboarding as well?"

"Thanks Tony, I'm into sports on rolls and boards, like skating, skateboarding, snowboarding and skiing. But I like riding bicycles the most." Stacy said with a smile on her face.

"Wow. For me, I'm a big fan of ball games. Football, basketball and volleyball are the three most famous ball games in the world, but I'm more interested in some 'small balls'. Baseball, my favourite sport, is very popular in America and Japan. Table tennis and badminton are popular in China."

"And tennis is well known in the world! My mum is a successful tennis player and she won the first prize in one of the Olympic Games. She gave me a racket. But it's really hard for me to play tennis."

"Cricket, golf and ice hockey are also very popular. You can try them."

"You are really a young expert in ball games, Tony. But I'm afraid the cricket bat is too heavy to play long. I can try golf and ice hockey. In addition, it's very important to prepare sports kit before we do sports, such as swimsuits for swimming, a pair of special shoes for climbing and a life jacket for sailing."

"Right. We also need litres of water and several kilos of chocolate in case of energy loss."

"Kilos of chocolate? Sure? Fifty grammes; that's enough."

"Sorry, I'm also a big fan of chocolate." Tony and Stacy laughed happily.

两个运动迷

参考译文

托尼在体育中心休息时遇到了斯黛西。

"斯黛西,你滑冰滑得好棒!你是不是也擅长滑板呀?"

"谢谢你,托尼,我喜欢轮上和板上运动,比如滑冰、滑板运动、滑雪板运动和滑雪运动。但是我最喜欢骑自行车。"斯黛西笑着说道。

"哇。我一直是个球类运动迷。足球、篮球和排球是全世界最知名的三大球类运动,但我对一些'小球'更感兴趣。我最喜欢的棒球运动在美国和日本非常受欢迎,乒乓球和羽毛球运动在中国很流行。"

"网球运动在全世界都很流行!我妈妈就是一名成功的网球运动员,她曾在一届奥运会上得了第一名。她送了我一副球拍,但是对我来说打网球真的很难。"

"板球、高尔夫和冰球也很流行。你可以试试。"

"托尼,你真是个小小球类运动专家。但是恐怕板球板太重,我打不了太久。我倒是可以试试高尔夫球和冰球。此外,在运动前准备好运动装备也是非常重要的!比如游泳要准备泳衣,攀岩要准备一双特殊的鞋子,帆船运动要准备救生衣。"

"是的,我们还需要几升水和几千克巧克力以防能量缺失。"

"几千克巧克力?你确定吗?50 克足够了。"

"抱歉,我也是个巧克力迷。"托尼和斯黛西开心地笑了。

Word list

rest [rest] v. & n. 休息

sports centre 体育中心

skate [skeɪt] v. 滑冰;溜冰

skateboarding [ˈskeɪtbɔːdɪŋ] n. 滑板运动
联想 skateboard n. 滑板

skating [ˈskeɪtɪŋ] n. 滑冰;溜冰
搭配 go (ice) skating 去滑冰

snowboarding [ˈsnəʊbɔːdɪŋ] n. 滑雪板运动
联想 snowboard n. 滑雪板

skiing [ˈskiːɪŋ] n. 滑雪(运动)
联想 ski v. 滑雪
搭配 go skiing 去滑雪

ride [raɪd] v. 骑,乘 n.(乘车或骑车的)短途旅程(过去式 rode;过去分词 ridden)
搭配 ride a bicycle 骑自行车
联想 riding n. 骑马

bicycle [ˈbaɪsɪkl] n. 自行车
联想 tricycle n. 三轮车
同义 bike 自行车

basketball [ˈbɑːskɪtbɔːl] n. 篮球

volleyball [ˈvɒlibɔːl] n. 排球

baseball [ˈbeɪsbɔːl] n. 棒球

table tennis 乒乓球(英式)
同义 ping-pong 乒乓球(美式)

070

Day 12

badminton [ˈbædmɪntən] n. 羽毛球运动

tennis [ˈtenɪs] n. 网球运动

well known 众所周知的；出名的
例句 His books are not well known. 他写的书不太有名。
注意 well known 用于修饰人或物时，中间需加连字符，比如：a well-known actor 著名演员。

successful [səkˈsesfl] adj. 成功的
搭配 be successful in 在……方面成功

tennis player 网球选手

prize [praɪz] n. 奖；奖品
搭配 first prize 一等奖

racket [ˈrækɪt] n. 球拍
搭配 tennis rackets 网球拍

hard [hɑːd] adj. 困难的；努力的（比较级 harder；最高级 hardest）

cricket [ˈkrɪkɪt] n. 板球（运动）
搭配 a cricket match 板球比赛

golf [ɡɒlf] n. 高尔夫球运动

hockey [ˈhɒki] n. 曲棍球；冰球
搭配 ice hockey 冰球运动
注意 英式英语中意为"曲棍球"，美式英语中意为"冰球"。

young [jʌŋ] adj. 年轻的；幼小的

搭配 young football players 年轻的足球运动员

bat [bæt] n. 球棒；球板
搭配 a cricket bat 板球球板

heavy [ˈhevi] adj. 重的；沉的

important [ɪmˈpɔːtnt] adj. 重要的；有重大影响的

kit [kɪt] n. 全套衣服及装备；成套工具
搭配 sports kit 运动用品

swimsuit [ˈswɪmsuːt] n. 泳衣
助记 swim（游泳）+ suit（套装）
同义 swimming costume 泳衣

climbing [ˈklaɪmɪŋ] n. 登山运动
注意 其中 b 不发音。
联想 climb v. 攀登；爬
搭配 go climbing 去登山

sailing [ˈseɪlɪŋ] n. 航行；帆船运动
联想 sail v. 航行
例句 Do you go sailing often? 你经常出海航行吗？

litre [ˈliːtə(r)] n. 升（英式）
注意 美式英语拼写为 liter。

kilo [ˈkiːləʊ] n. 公斤；千克（单位符号：kg）
全称 kilogram(me) 公斤；千克

gramme [ɡræm] n. 克（英式）
注意 美式英语拼写为 gram。

Exercise

1. Listen and read these phrases and sentences aloud.

   1. football, basketball and volleyball
   2. a successful tennis player
   3. win the first prize

4. tennis racket and cricket bat

5. skateboarding and snowboarding

6. Susan is good at swimming instead of riding bicycles.

7. Kobe was a well-known basketball player in America.

8. When I was young, I was crazy about badminton.

9. We need to prepare sports kit for that skiing race.

10. I've bought 3 litres of milk and 2 kilos of potatoes in the market.

II. Label the pictures.

1. b_____   2. v_____   3. t____ t_____

4. b_____   5. t_____   6. b_____

7. s_____   8. s____   9. b_____   10. c_____

III. Listen and choose the correct answer for each question.

1. Where does the man come from?
   A. England.   B. Canada.   C. Singapore.

2. Which sport does the woman like the most?
   A. Baseball.   B. Tennis.   C. Table tennis.

3. When will they meet in the sports centre on Sunday?

   A. At 10 a. m.　　　　B. At 2 p. m.　　　　C. At 8 p. m.

IV. Answer the questions.

1. Which sport do you want to try most? Why?

   _____

   _____

2. Have you ever joined a sports team?

   _____

   _____

3. What will you put in your sports kit when you're doing sport?

   _____

   _____

Unit 7
Hobbies and Jobs

Pre-test

快速浏览下面的单词，自测一下，看看你是否已经掌握了呢？记得标记你不熟悉的单词，多多复习哦！

- [ ] act　　　　　　[ækt] v. 表演 n. 行为
- [ ] disco　　　　　['dɪskəʊ] n. 迪斯科舞厅
- [ ] quiz　　　　　　[kwɪz] n. 测试；知识竞赛
- [ ] circle　　　　　['sɜːkl] n. 圆圈
- [ ] circus　　　　　['sɜːkəs] n. 马戏团
- [ ] king　　　　　　[kɪŋ] n. 君主；国王
- [ ] queen　　　　　[kwiːn] n. 女王；王后
- [ ] secretary　　　['sekrətri] n. 秘书
- [ ] boss　　　　　　[bɒs] n. 老板
- [ ] manager　　　　['mænɪdʒə(r)] n. 经理，经营者
- [ ] business　　　　['bɪznəs] n. 商业；生意
- [ ] staff　　　　　　[stɑːf] n. 全体职工
- [ ] cleaner　　　　　['kliːnə(r)] n. 清洁工
- [ ] footballer　　　　['fʊtbɔːlə(r)] n. （职业）足球运动员
- [ ] football player　　足球运动员
- [ ] cook　　　　　　[kʊk] v. 烹饪 n. 厨师
- [ ] worker　　　　　['wɜːkə(r)] n. 工人
- [ ] police　　　　　　[pəˈliːs] n. 警察
- [ ] police car　　　　警车
- [ ] might　　　　　　[maɪt] mv. 可能，可以
- [ ] can　　　　　　　[kæn] mv. 能，会
- [ ] could　　　　　　[kʊd] mv. 能，可以
- [ ] kite　　　　　　　[kaɪt] n. 风筝

故事导读：
1. 小朋友，试着找出 Alice 和她的朋友们都有什么爱好吧。
2. 记得标记出新学到的单词和句式哦。

Hobbies Make Our Life Interesting

Alice made lots of new friends in the new school. She invited her friends Lily, Dan and Richard to her home on Sunday.

Alice's friends came to her room. There were several **toys** and **dolls** on the shelf. A **stamp album** on the desk was noticed by Lily.

Lily pointed at it and asked Alice, "You like **collecting** stamps, right?"

"Yes. I also like **painting** and **photographing** to record the beauty of the daily life," answered Alice and then she asked, "What are your **hobbies**, guys?"

"Actually I like **listening to classical music played** by the **violin** and **piano** and going to the **opera**. But last week my father took me to a **rock** concert. A rock **band** made me interested. When the **singer sang songs**, the other members in the band played the **musical instruments** like the **guitar, drums**. So now I also enjoy listening to rock music. In the future, I hope to be a **musician**," answered Richard quickly.

Lily is a girl who is very **active**. She answered, "Wow, you like **art**, but I am interested in taking **adventures**. I love going **camping** with my parents. It is so wonderful to be surrounded by nature."

Dan is a quiet boy. He said, "Sounds **fun**! But I prefer to **read newspapers, magazines, comics** and **draw pictures**."

"I watch **cartoon films** sometimes. We should play together more often. What about playing **cards** or board **games** like **chess** next weekend?" said Richard.

"Great! I will get bored without you guys. It is so lucky to have you to be my friends." Alice spoke out her feelings excitedly.

爱好使我们的生活有趣

参考译文

爱丽丝在新学校交了很多新朋友。她邀请了她的朋友莉莉、丹和理查德星期天到她家。

爱丽丝的朋友们来到了她的房间里。房间的架子上有几个玩具和娃娃。莉莉注意到了书桌上的一本集邮册。

莉莉指着集邮册问爱丽丝:"你喜欢集邮,是吗?"

"是的,我喜欢集邮。我还喜欢绘画和摄影,记录日常生活中的美好事物。"爱丽丝回答说,随后她问道:"你们的爱好是什么呢?"

"事实上,我喜欢听小提琴和钢琴演奏的古典音乐,还喜欢去听歌剧。但是上周我爸爸带我去听了一场摇滚音乐会。我对其中的一支摇滚乐队很感兴趣。歌手演唱时,乐队其他成员会演奏吉他、鼓之类的乐器。所以现在我也喜欢听摇滚乐。我希望自己将来能成为一名音乐家。"理查德迅速答道。

莉莉是一个非常活跃的女孩。她回答说:"哇,你喜欢艺术,但我感兴趣的是冒险。我喜欢和爸爸妈妈去露营。身处大自然的感觉非常美妙。"

丹是一个安静的男孩。他说:"听起来很有趣!但是我更喜欢看报纸、杂志和漫画,我还喜欢画画。"

"我有时观看卡通电影。我们应该经常在一起玩。下周末打牌或者玩国际象棋之类的棋类游戏怎么样?"理查德说。

"太棒了!没有你们我会很无聊。真幸运有你们做我的朋友。"爱丽丝兴奋地说出了自己的感受。

Word list

toy [tɔɪ] n. 玩具

doll [dɒl] n. 玩偶;玩具娃娃

stamp [stæmp] n. 邮票
搭配 a stamp album 集邮册

album [ˈælbəm] n. 相册;影集
搭配 a photo album 相册

collect [kəˈlekt] v. 收集;收藏
搭配 collect stamps 集邮

paint [peɪnt] v. 用颜料画
例句 A friend painted the children for me. 一位朋友给我画了孩子们的画像。

photograph [ˈfəʊtəɡrɑːf] v. 拍照 n. 照片
搭配 take photographs 拍照

hobby [ˈhɒbi] n. 业余爱好
例句 Her hobby is swimming. 她爱好游泳。

actually [ˈæktʃuəli] adv. 真实地；事实上

listen to 听……；听从
例句 I love listening to music. 我喜欢听音乐。

classical [ˈklæsɪkl] adj. 古典的；经典的

music [ˈmjuːzɪk] n. 音乐；乐曲
搭配 classical music 古典音乐

play [pleɪ] v. 演奏；玩耍

violin [ˌvaɪəˈlɪn] n. 小提琴
搭配 play the violin 拉小提琴

piano [piˈænəʊ] n. 钢琴
搭配 play the piano 弹钢琴

opera [ˈɒprə] n. 歌剧
搭配 go to the opera 去看歌剧

rock [rɒk] n. 摇滚乐

band [bænd] n. 流行音乐乐队
搭配 a rock band 摇滚乐队

singer [ˈsɪŋə(r)] n. 歌唱家；歌手
例句 She's a wonderful singer. 她唱歌唱得非常好。

sing [sɪŋ] v. 唱；演唱（过去式 sang；过去分词 sung）
例句 Will you sing us a song? 你给我们唱支歌好吗？

song [sɒŋ] n. 歌；歌曲
例句 We sang a song together. 我们一起唱了一首歌。

musical [ˈmjuːzɪkl] adj. 音乐的；有音乐的

instrument [ˈɪnstrəmənt] n. 乐器
搭配 a musical instrument 乐器

guitar [ɡɪˈtɑː(r)] n. 吉他

drum [drʌm] n. 鼓

musician [mjuˈzɪʃn] n. 音乐家
搭配 a famous musician 著名的音乐家

active [ˈæktɪv] adj. 活跃的；积极的
搭配 take an active part in 积极参加

art [ɑːt] n. 艺术，美术

adventure [ədˈventʃə(r)] n. 冒险；冒险经历
搭配 adventure stories 历险故事

camping [ˈkæmpɪŋ] n. 野营度假
例句 Do you go camping? 你去野营度假吗？

fun [fʌn] n. 享乐；乐趣 adj. 有趣的
例句 Have fun! 尽情地玩吧！

read [riːd] v. 阅读（过去式和过去分词 read）

newspaper [ˈnjuːzpeɪpə(r)] n. 报纸

magazine [ˌmæɡəˈziːn] n. 杂志；期刊

comic [ˈkɒmɪk] n. 连环画杂志

draw [drɔː] v. 画

picture [ˈpɪktʃə(r)] n. 图画；照片
搭配 draw pictures 画画

cartoon [kɑːˈtuːn] n. 动画片；卡通片

film [fɪlm] n. 电影；影片（英式）
同义 movie 电影（美式）
搭配 a cartoon film 动画电影
a film star 电影明星

card [kɑːd] n. 卡片
搭配 card games 纸牌游戏

game [ɡeɪm] n. 游戏
搭配 board games 棋类游戏

chess [tʃes] n. 国际象棋

bored [bɔːd] adj. 厌倦的；烦闷的
搭配 be bored with 对……厌烦

Exercise

I. Listen and read the phrases and sentence aloud.

1. toys and dolls
2. listen to classical music
3. violin, guitar, piano and drum
4. collect stamps
5. What is your hobby?
6. read newspapers and draw pictures
7. go camping
8. sing a song
9. cartoon films
10. card games and board games

II. Label the pictures.

1. c_ _ _ _
2. s_ _ _ _
3. g_ _ _ _ _
4. m_ _ _ _
5. v_ _ _ _ _
6. s_ _ _
7. r_ _ _
8. d_ _ _
9. p_ _ _ _
10. f_ _ _

III. Listen and choose the correct answer for each question.

1. How often does Tommy have his guitar lessons?

    A. Once a week.　　　B. Twice a week.　　　C. Three times a week.

2. Which instrument can Amy play?

   A. The guitar.　　　B. The violin.　　　C. The drum.

3. Who is good at music?

   A. Amy's father.　　B. Amy's mother.　　C. Tommy's father.

IV. **Answer the questions.**

1. What is your hobby?

   _____

   _____

2. What is your best friend's hobby?

   _____

   _____

3. Do you know your father's or your mother's hobbies?

   _____

   _____

故事导读：
1. 小朋友，你的梦想是什么？你长大以后想做什么呢？
2. 记得标记出新学到的单词和句式哦。

What Is Your Future Career?

Maria and Jessica are classmates. They need to finish an art project. On Sunday they went to an exhibition of the famous painter and artist Picasso and found some materials. Maria took some beautiful pictures with her camera.

"Wow, good job. What is your future career? A photographer, right?" asked Jessica curiously.

"No. My mother is a dancer. She dances well. When I was a child, I wanted to be a dancer like her. But when I grow up, I know that my father and his colleagues' work is respected by people and they can save lots of people's lives. So now I want to be a rescue pilot like them," answered Maria.

Then she added, "I want to tell you the story about my parents. They have a common interest in music. They both like pop, hip hop, jazz and rap. They first met at a concert of Beyonce. When watching her shows, they knew each other. Finally, they got married."

"Oh, your parents' story sounds like a love comedy. Well, my father used to be a mechanic, but now he is an engineer. Although he cannot earn much money like a businessman or an actor, he can get enough for us to have a comfortable life. I used to dream of being a writer or journalist to record common people's lives. However, after I saw my grandfather recover from a serious illness because of the help offered by doctors and nurses, I decided to become a doctor," answered Jessica.

Maria looked very excited and said, "That's great! Other occupations like teachers, dentists, drivers, or police officers are also great jobs."

你的未来职业是什么呢？

参考译文

玛丽亚和杰西卡是同班同学。他们需要完成一项艺术专题研究。星期天，她们去参观了著名画家和艺术家——毕加索的展览，寻找了一些素材。玛丽亚用她的相机拍了一些漂亮的照片。

"哇，拍得真好。你的未来职业是什么？是成为一名摄影师，对吗？"杰西卡好奇地问。

"不。我妈妈是一名舞蹈家。她的舞跳得很好。当我还是个孩子的时候，我想成为一名像她一样的舞者。但是当我长大后，我得知父亲和他的同事们的工作很受人尊敬，他们可以挽救很多人的生命。所以现在我想成为一名像他们一样的救援飞行员。"玛丽亚回答道。

然后她补充道："我想告诉你关于我父母的故事。他们对音乐有着共同的爱好。他们都喜欢流行音乐、嘻哈音乐、爵士乐和说唱乐。他们第一次见面是在碧昂斯的音乐会上。在看她的演出时，他们相识了。最后，他们结婚了。"

"哦，你父母的故事听起来就像一部爱情喜剧。嗯，我父亲过去是一名机械师，但现在他是一名工程师。虽然他不能像商人或演员那样赚很多钱，但他挣的钱足以让我们过上舒适的生活。我曾经梦想成为一名作家或记者，来记录普通人的生活。然而，当我看到爷爷在医生和护士的帮助下从一场重病中康复后，我决定成为一名医生。"杰西卡回答说。

玛丽亚看起来很兴奋，说道："太好了！其他职业比如教师、牙医、司机或警察也很不错。"

Word list

need [niːd] v. 需要
例句 I need to get some sleep. 我需要睡会儿觉。

project [ˈprɒdʒekt] n. 专题研究；项目
搭配 a history project 历史专题研究

exhibition [ˌeksɪˈbɪʃn] n. 展览
例句 Have you ever been to the Picasso exhibition? 你去过毕加索的画展吗？

painter [ˈpeɪntə(r)] n. 画家
搭配 a famous painter 著名的画家

artist [ˈɑːtɪst] n. 艺术家
搭配 a great artist 伟大的艺术家

camera [ˈkæmərə] n. 照相机
搭配 a digital camera 数码相机

job [dʒɒb] n. 工作；任务
例句 Good job! 干得不错！

career [kəˈrɪə(r)] n. 生涯；职业
搭配 a change of career 调换职业

photographer [fəˈtɒɡrəfə(r)] n. 拍照者；摄影师

搭配 a fashion photographer 时装摄影师

dancer [ˈdɑːnsə(r)] n. 跳舞者；舞蹈演员

dance [dɑːns] v. & n. 跳舞
例句 Do you want to dance? 你想跳舞吗？

colleague [ˈkɒliːɡ] n. 同事
搭配 a colleague of mine from the office 我办公室的一位同事

work [wɜːk] n. 工作；职业
例句 I'm still looking for work. 我仍在找工作。

pilot [ˈpaɪlət] n. 飞行员
搭配 a rescue pilot 救援飞行员

pop [pɒp] adj. 流行音乐的 n. 流行音乐
搭配 pop music 流行音乐

hip hop 嘻哈舞曲

jazz [dʒæz] n. 爵士乐

rap [ræp] n. 说唱音乐

concert [ˈkɒnsət] n. 音乐会
搭配 a pop concert 流行音乐会

show [ʃəʊ] n. 演出 v. 展示
例句 She's the star of the show! 她是这场演出的明星！

comedy [ˈkɒmədi] n. 喜剧；喜剧片
搭配 a love comedy 爱情喜剧片

mechanic [məˈkænɪk] n. 机械师；机械修理工
搭配 a car mechanic 汽车修理工

engineer [ˌendʒɪˈnɪə(r)] n. 工程师

cannot [ˈkænɒt] mv. 不能；不可 (= can't)
例句 I cannot believe the price of the tickets! 我简直无法相信竟有这样的票价！

earn [ɜːn] v. 挣得；赚得
例句 He earns about $40,000 a year. 他一年大约挣4万美元。

businessman [ˈbɪznəsmæn] n. （男）商人
助记 business（商业）+ man（男人）
联想 businesswoman n. 女商人

actor [ˈæktə(r)] n. 演员
搭配 a poor actor 差劲的演员
联想 actress n. 女演员

comfortable [ˈkʌmftəbl] adj. 舒服的；安逸的
例句 Are you comfortable? 你感觉舒服吗？

writer [ˈraɪtə(r)] n. 作家；作者
搭配 a travel writer 游记作家

journalist [ˈdʒɜːnəlɪst] n. 新闻记者；新闻工作者
搭配 a famous journalist 有名的记者

offer [ˈɒfə(r)] v. 提供；自愿给予
例句 They decided to offer the job to Joe. 他们决定提供乔这份工作。

doctor [ˈdɒktə(r)] n. 医生；大夫（缩写 Dr）

nurse [nɜːs] n. 护士

occupation [ˌɒkjuˈpeɪʃn] n. 工作；职业
例句 What is your occupation? 你的职业是什么？

teacher [ˈtiːtʃə(r)] n. 教师；老师
搭配 a good teacher 优秀的教师

dentist [ˈdentɪst] n. 牙科医生

driver [ˈdraɪvə(r)] n. 驾驶员；司机
搭配 a driver's licence 驾照

police officer 警察

Day 14

Exercise

Ⅰ. Listen and read the phrases and sentence aloud.

1. a famous painter and artist's exhibition
2. a pop concert
3. hip hop, jazz and rap
4. mechanic and engineer
5. What is your occupation?
6. a love comedy
7. earn much money
8. doctors and nurses
9. driver, writer, teacher and police officer
10. dentist and journalist

Ⅱ. Label the pictures.

1. p_ _ _ _ _ o_ _ _ _ _ _

2. d_ _ _ _ _

3. p_ _ _ _ _ _

4. t_ _ _ _ _ _

5. b_ _ _ _ _ _ _ _ _ _

6. w_ _ _ _ _

7. d _ _ _ _ _   8. p _ _ _ _   9. m _ _ _ _ _ _ _

10. e _ _ _ _ _ _ _   11. a _ _ _ _   12. j _ _ _ _ _ _ _ _

Ⅲ. Listen and then match the names and careers.

Names
1. Rose ☐
2. Tony ☐
3. Amy   ☐

Careers
A. dentist
B. teacher
C. writer
D. journalist

Ⅳ. Read the email from your English friend, Jack.

From:	Jack
To:	

Today I told my classmates that singing and dancing are my hobbies and I want to be a musician in the future.

What's your hobby? What career will you choose in the future? And why?

Write an email to Jack and answer the questions.

Write **25 words** and more.

_____

_____

_____

_____

Unit 8
Places and Buildings

Pre-test

快速浏览下面的单词，自测一下，看看你是否已经掌握了呢？记得标记你不熟悉的单词，多多复习哦！

- ☐ address [ə'dres] n. 地址
- ☐ petrol station 加油站（英式）
- ☐ gas station 加油站（美式）
- ☐ port [pɔːt] n. 港口
- ☐ park [pɑːk] n. 公园 v. 停（车）
- ☐ beach [biːtʃ] n. 海滩；沙滩
- ☐ ugly ['ʌgli] adj. 丑陋的；难看的
- ☐ dangerous ['deɪndʒərəs] adj. 有危险的；不安全的
- ☐ path [pɑːθ] n. 小路
- ☐ farm [fɑːm] n. 农场
- ☐ farmer ['fɑːmə(r)] n. 农场主
- ☐ factory ['fæktəri] n. 工厂
- ☐ noise [nɔɪz] n. 噪音
- ☐ round [raʊnd] adj. 圆形的
- ☐ above [ə'bʌv] adv. & prep. 在……上面
- ☐ over ['əʊvə(r)] prep. & adv. 在……上面
- ☐ under ['ʌndə(r)] prep. 在……下面
- ☐ below [bɪ'ləʊ] adv. & prep. 在……下面
- ☐ against [ə'geɪnst] prep. 靠着
- ☐ surprise [sə'praɪz] v. 使惊奇；使诧异
- ☐ apartment building 公寓大楼

Day 15

故事导读：
1. 小朋友，你知道大学是什么样的吗？跟着 Thomas 一起在大学校园里转转吧。
2. 遇到表示方位的单词，记得标记出来哦。

A Campus Walking Tour（1）

Good morning! Thank you for attending the Open Day. My name is Thomas and I'm your guide. I'll show you around the university today. There're many visitors on campus, so please just follow me and don't get lost in the crowd.

We're now at the south entrance. This is where the tour begins. Walk along East Street for about two minutes and turn right at Albert Way, and then we can see the building of the business school at the corner of the roads. It was newly built last year and it's a beautiful architecture. The statue in front of the building is a famous economist who graduated from this school.

Facing north, we can see the building of social science departments on the left-hand side, the engineering school on the right-hand side, and the medical school in between. Behind the three buildings, there is a museum which is operated by the university. All the exhibitions are free for students. On the opposite side of the road, there is a big car park which is also open to the public.

Keep walking straight and then cross the bridge. The tall building on your left is the library. Its entrance is on the first floor. There's a cafeteria downstairs where students can have lunch. I'm sorry that we cannot go inside because students need a quiet reading environment, but we can have a look at the map beside the lifts. The space for group work and self-learning are all upstairs. Looking out of west windows, you can see a football stadium and a playground.

校园步行游（一）

参考译文

早上好！谢谢大家来参加校园开放日。我是托马斯，你们的导游。今天我会带领大家参观这所大学。今天校园里有很多访客，所以请你们紧跟着我，不要在人群中走散了。

我们现在位于南入口，参观将会从这里开始。沿着东大街向前走大约两分钟，然后在阿尔伯特路向右转，我们会看到坐落于两条路夹角处的商学院大楼。它是去年才新修建的，是一栋非常美丽的建筑。楼前的雕像是一位著名的经济学家，他毕业于这所大学。

面向北边，我们可以看到社会科学学院的大楼在我们的左边，工程学院的大楼在我们的右边，而医学院大楼在这两栋楼之间。在这三座建筑的后面，有一座由学校运营的博物馆。所有的展览都对学生免费开放。在路的对面有一个大型停车场，也是对公众开放的。

继续向前直走，然后过桥，你们左边的大楼是图书馆。图书馆入口位于二层。楼下有一个食堂，学生们可以在这里吃午餐。很抱歉我们没法进入图书馆内部，因为学生们需要安静的阅读环境，但是我们可以看一下电梯旁边的地图。小组讨论区和自习区都在楼上。从西面的窗户往外看，你们可以看到一个足球场和一个操场。

Word list

guide [gaɪd] *n.* 指南；导游
搭配 a tour guide 导游

around [ə'raʊnd] *adv.* 四周；周围 *prep.* 围绕
例句 The children were around her. 孩子们在她周围。

crowd [kraʊd] *n.* 人群
例句 He pushed his way through the crowd. 他在人群中往前挤。

south [saʊθ] *n.* 南方 *adj.* 南方的 *adv.* 朝南
例句 This house faces south. 这间屋子朝南。

entrance ['entrəns] *n.* 入口；大门
搭配 the front/back/side entrance of the house 房子的前门/后门/侧门

where [weə(r)] *adv.* 在哪里
例句 Where do you live? 你住在哪儿？

walk [wɔːk] *v.* 走，步行；散步
搭配 walk around the streets 在大街上闲逛

along [ə'lɒŋ] *prep.* 沿着；顺着
例句 They walked slowly along the road. 他们沿着公路慢慢走。

east [iːst] *n.* 东方 *adj.* 东方的 *adv.* 朝东
搭配 a town to the east of Chicago 芝加哥以东的一个城镇

street [striːt] *n.* 街道
例句 The bank is just across the street. 银行就在街道对面。

right [raɪt] *adj.* 正确的；右边的 *n.* 正确；右边
例句 Keep on the right side of the road. 靠马路右边行走。

building ['bɪldɪŋ] *n.* 建筑；建筑物
搭配 historic buildings 有历史意义的建筑物

corner ['kɔːnə(r)] *n.* 角落；拐角处
例句 There is a boy standing on the street corner. 有一个男孩站在街角。

road [rəud] *n.* 公路，马路；道路
搭配 a country road 乡村道路

build [bɪld] *v.* 建立；建筑（过去式/过去分词 built）
搭配 a house built of stone 用石头建造的房子

beautiful [ˈbjuːtɪfl] *adj.* 美丽的
反义 ugly 丑陋的

front [frʌnt] *n.* 前面；正面
搭配 in front of 在……前面

north [nɔːθ] *n.* 北方 *adj.* 北方的 *adv.* 朝北
例句 Which way is north? 哪边是北方？

left-hand [ˈleft hænd] *adj.* 左手的；左边的
搭配 the left-hand side of the street 街的左侧

right-hand [ˈraɪt hænd] *adj.* 右手的；右边的
搭配 a right-hand glove 右手的手套

side [saɪd] *n.* 侧面；一侧
例句 She is on the far side of the room. 她在房间的那一边。

between [bɪˈtwiːn] *prep.* 在……之间
搭配 between two trees 在两棵树之间

behind [bɪˈhaɪnd] *adv. & prep.* 在……后面
例句 Who's the girl standing behind Jane? 站在简身后的女孩是谁？

museum [mjuˈziːəm] *n.* 博物馆
搭配 a science museum 科学博物馆

opposite [ˈɒpəzɪt] *prep.* 在……对面
例句 The bank is opposite the supermarket. 银行在超市对面。

big [bɪg] *adj.* 大的

car park 停车场（英式）
同义 parking lot 停车场（美式）

straight [streɪt] *adj.* 直的 *adv.* 笔直地
例句 Keep straight on for two miles. 一直向前走两英里。

cross [krɒs] *v.* 穿越；越过

bridge [brɪdʒ] *n.* 桥
搭配 cross the bridge 过桥

tall [tɔːl] *adj.* 高的（比较级 taller；最高级 tallest）
搭配 the tallest building in the world 世界上最高的建筑物

left [left] *adj.* 左边的 *n.* 左边
搭配 the left side 左边

library [ˈlaɪbrəri] *n.* 图书馆
搭配 a public library 公共图书馆

downstairs [ˌdaʊnˈsteəz] *adv.* 在楼下
助记 down（向下）+stairs（楼梯）

inside [ˌɪnˈsaɪd] *adv. & prep.* 在……里面
例句 Go inside the house. 进屋吧。

quiet [ˈkwaɪət] *adj.* 安静的
搭配 a quiet street 寂静的街道

map [mæp] *n.* 地图
搭配 read a map 查看地图

beside [bɪˈsaɪd] *prep.* 在旁边
搭配 He sat beside her all night. 整个晚上他都坐在她身边。

lift [lɪft] *n.* 电梯（英式）
例句 Take the lift to the third floor. 乘坐电梯去四楼。
同义 elevator 电梯（美式）

upstairs [ˌʌpˈsteəz] *adv.* 在楼上
助记 up（向上）+stairs（楼梯）
例句 I carried her bags upstairs. 我把她的包拿到了楼上。

out [aʊt] *adv.* （从……里）出来
搭配 look out of the window 向窗外看

west [west] *n.* 西方 *adj.* 西方的 *adv.* 朝西

stadium [ˈsteɪdiəm] *n.* 体育场；运动场
搭配 a football stadium 足球场

playground [ˈpleɪgraʊnd] *n.* 游戏场；操场
助记 play（玩耍）+ground（地面）

Exercise

I. Listen and read the phrases aloud.

1. north and south
2. east and west
3. left and right
4. left-hand and right-hand
5. inside and outside
6. upstairs and downstairs

II. Label the pictures.

1. n _ _ _ _   2. w _ _ _   5. l _ _ _   6. r _ _ _ _
3. s _ _ _ _   4. e _ _ _

7. f _ _ _ _   8. b _ _ _ _ _   9. u _ _ _ _ _ _ _
                                   10. d _ _ _ _ _ _ _ _ _

III. Listen and choose the correct answer for each question.

1. Where is Jamie?

A   B

2. Which building is the library?

A　　　　　　　　　　　B

3. Where are the kids now?

A　　　　　　　　　　　B

IV. Answer the questions.

1. Can you read a map?

_____

_____

2. In which directions does the sun rise and set?

_____

_____

3. Which direction does your home face?

_____

_____

故事导读：
1. 小朋友，你喜欢什么样的校园环境呢？来看看这是不是你理想中的校园吧。
2. 试着将表示建筑物的名词标记出来吧。

A Campus Walking Tour (2)

Going across the Edward Road, we arrive at the Student Union (SU). There's a grocery store, a bank, and a bookshop on the ground floor. The restaurant on the first floor is popular among students where they can have a drink outside at the balcony and enjoy the pretty view of the campus. Close to the SU, there's a large public square. It's sometimes crowded and noisy in the middle of the term when there are live campus sports events.

Walking through the square, you can see a grand building with a shining top. Are you surprised that this is the largest art centre in the country? It contains two cinemas, two theatres, and a gallery (画廊).

Now I'm going to show you the on-campus flats. There're nearly 1,000 rooms across four blocks. You can also live in hotels in the city centre, which is a few kilometres away. There're many bus stations, and students can take buses to and from campus in all directions. We'll build the underground next year.

In their spare time, students can visit close-by towns and villages with long histories. There's a famous castle built in the 11th century which is not far away from here. The nearest railway station is only 800 metres away and the capital city is just an hour's train ride. Within 20 minutes' drive, you can arrive at the airport. By the way, there're two supermarkets, a department store, a hospital and a police station nearby so it is very convenient and safe to live here.

It is a great place for students to enjoy their university life in the busy city and easy countryside.

校园步行游（二）

参考译文

穿过爱德华路，我们来到了学生活动大楼。一层有杂货店、银行和书店。位于二层的餐厅很受学生欢迎，他们可以在外面的露台上边喝饮料边欣赏校园美丽的景色。距离学生活动大楼不远处有一个很大的公共广场。在每学期的期中阶段，这里有时会直播校园体育赛事，那时这里就会拥挤嘈杂。

穿过广场，你可以看到一座顶部闪闪发光的宏伟建筑。得知它是全国最大的艺术中心，你会惊讶吗？这里有两家电影院、两家剧院，还有一个画廊。

现在我要带大家去看一下校园里的公寓楼。这里一共有将近1000个房间，分布在四栋大楼之中。你也可以住在几千米之外的市中心酒店。这里有很多公交车站，学生可以乘坐公共汽车往返于校园与各个地方。我们将在明年修建地铁。

课余时间里，学生们可以在附近参观历史悠久的城镇和村落。有一座修建于11世纪的著名古堡就在这附近。最近的火车站距离学校只有800米，去首都只需要乘坐一个小时的火车。驾车20分钟，你就可以抵达机场。顺便说一下，附近还有两家超市、一家百货商店、一家医院和一个警察局，所以说住在这里既方便又安全。

这里是让学生能够在繁忙的都市和悠闲的乡村享受大学生活的绝佳去处。

Word list

across [əˈkrɒs] *adv. & prep.* 穿过；在……对面
例句 The bank's across the road. 银行在马路对面。
He walked across the bridge. 他走过了这座桥。

grocery store 杂货店

bank [bæŋk] *n.* 银行
例句 I need to go to the bank. 我得去银行。

bookshop [ˈbʊkʃɒp] *n.* 书店（英式）
同义 bookstore 书店（美式）
助记 book（书）+shop（商店）

restaurant [ˈrestrɒnt] *n.* 餐馆
搭配 a Chinese restaurant 中餐厅

outside [ˌaʊtˈsaɪd] *adv. & prep.* 在外面；在户外
反义 inside 在里面
例句 Let's eat outside. 我们去外面吃饭吧。

pretty [ˈprɪti] *adj.* 漂亮的

view [vjuː] *n.* 意见；风景
搭配 a pretty sea view 漂亮的海景

close to 接近；靠近
搭配 close to the beaches 靠近海滩

large [lɑːdʒ] *adj.* 大的
搭配 a large house 大房子

square [skweə(r)] *n.* 广场；正方形
例句 The house is close to one of the city's prettiest squares. 这栋房子靠近市区最漂亮的广场之一。

crowded [ˈkraʊdɪd] *adj.* 拥挤的

读故事 巧记 KET 核心词汇

搭配 crowded streets 拥挤的街道

noisy [ˈnɔɪzi] *adj.* 嘈杂的；喧闹的
反义 quiet 安静的
例句 This area can be very noisy at night-time. 这个地方夜间有时会非常吵闹。

middle [ˈmɪdl] *n.* 中间 *adj.* 中间的
例句 Bob's the one in the middle of the photo. 鲍勃是照片中间的那个人。

through [θruː] *adv. & prep.* 穿过
例句 The path led through the trees to the river. 这条小路穿过树林通向河边。

top [tɒp] *n.* 顶端
例句 Write your name at the top. 把你的姓名写在最上方。

surprised [səˈpraɪzd] *adj.* 感到惊讶的，出人意料的
例句 She looked surprised when I told her the fact. 当我告诉她事实时，她显得很惊讶。

country [ˈkʌntri] *n.* 国家；农村
搭配 European countries 欧洲国家

cinema [ˈsɪnəmə] *n.* 电影院
搭配 the local cinema 当地的电影院
go to the cinema（去电影院）看电影
同义 movie theatre 电影院（美式）

theatre [ˈθɪətə(r)] *n.* 戏院；剧场
搭配 Broadway theatres 百老汇剧院
注意 美式英语拼写为 theater。

flat [flæt] *n.* 公寓（英式）
同义 apartment 公寓（美式）
例句 Do you live in a flat or a house? 你住的是公寓还是独立住宅？

nearly [ˈnɪəli] *adv.* 差不多，几乎
例句 It's nearly time to leave. 差不多该走了。

block [blɒk] *n.* 大楼；一栋楼房
搭配 an office block 办公大楼

hotel [həʊˈtel] *n.* 旅馆
搭配 a five-star hotel 五星级宾馆

city [ˈsɪti] *n.* 城市，都市
搭配 the city centre 市中心

centre [ˈsentə(r)] *n.* 中心
搭配 in the centre of 在……中心

kilometre [ˈkɪləmiːtə(r)] *n.* 公里；千米
助记 kilo（千）+metre（米）
注意 美式英语拼写为 kilometer。

bus station 公交车站（英式）
同义 bus stop 公交车站（美式）

direction [dəˈrekʃn] *n.* 方向
例句 Tom went off in the direction of the square. 汤姆朝广场那边走去了。

underground [ˈʌndəɡraʊnd] *n.* 地铁（英式）
搭配 underground stations 地铁站
同义 subway 地铁（美式）

town [taʊn] *n.* 镇；城镇
例句 It's a ten-minute bus ride from here to town. 从这里到镇上乘坐公共汽车要花10分钟。

village [ˈvɪlɪdʒ] *n.* 村庄
搭配 a mountain village 山村

castle [ˈkɑːsl] *n.* 城堡

railway station 火车站

metre [ˈmiːtə(r)] *n.* 米

capital [ˈkæpɪtl] *n.* 首都
例句 Beijing is the capital of China. 北京是中国的首都。

airport [ˈeəpɔːt] *n.* 机场
搭配 the international airport 国际机场

Day 16

supermarket ['su:pəmɑ:kɪt] n. 超市
助记 super（超级的）+ market（市场）

department store 百货公司；百货商店

hospital ['hɒspɪtl] n. 医院
例句 I have to go to hospital. 我得去医院看病。

police station 警察局；派出所

safe [seɪf] adj. 安全的
反义 dangerous 危险的

great [greɪt] adj. 极大的；极好的

place [pleɪs] n. 地方；地点
例句 This would be a good place for a picnic. 这是野餐的好地方。

countryside ['kʌntrisaɪd] n. 乡村
助记 country（国家）+ side（边）
搭配 in the countryside 在乡村

Exercise

I. Listen and read the phrases aloud.

1. town and village
2. city and countryside
3. cinema and theatre
4. grocery store and department store
5. railway station and bus station
6. crowded and noisy
7. flat and hotel

II. Match the words with pictures.

Group 1

1.    A. cinema
2.    B. underground station
3.   C. railway station
4.    D. theatre
5.  E. bus station

Group 2

1.    A. bookshop
2.    B. hospital
3.    C. supermarket
4.  D. restaurant
5.  E. bank

III. Listen and choose the correct answer for each question.

1. Which bus should the boy take?
   A. Bus 11.   B. Bus 12.   C. Bus 13.
2. Where will the speakers meet?
   A. At the north gate.   B. At the west gate.   C. At the east gate.
3. Where is the girl's mum going this afternoon?
   A. To the hospital.   B. To the grocery store.   C. To the bookshop.

IV. Look at the three pictures.

Write the story shown in the pictures.

Write **35 words** or more.

_____

_____

_____

_____

Unit 9
Technology

Pre-test

快速浏览下面的单词,自测一下,看看你是否已经掌握了呢?记得标记你不熟悉的单词,多多复习哦!

- [ ] man [mæn] n. 男人
- [ ] woman ['wʊmən] n. 女人
- [ ] day [deɪ] n. 一天;白天
- [ ] PC (=personal computer) 个人电脑
- [ ] at/@ [æt] prep. 用于电子邮箱地址中的符号
- [ ] dot [dɒt] n. 点(电子邮件地址的组成部分)
- [ ] net [net] n. 网
- [ ] machine [məˈʃiːn] n. 机器
- [ ] site [saɪt] n. 网站
- [ ] such [sʌtʃ] det. 这样的;如此的
- [ ] no [nəʊ] adv. 不 det. 没有
- [ ] all [ɔːl] adv. 完全 det. 所有的 pron. 所有
- [ ] all kinds of 各种各样的
- [ ] all sorts of 各种各样的
- [ ] double [ˈdʌbl] adj. 两倍的
- [ ] check [tʃek] v. 检查;核查
- [ ] case [keɪs] n. 事例;容器
- [ ] ever [ˈevə(r)] adv. 曾经
- [ ] please [pliːz] v. 使愉快 exclam. 请
- [ ] from [frɒm] prep. 从……起,始于
- [ ] yet [jet] adv. 尚未;还
- [ ] thin [θɪn] adj. 薄的;细的
- [ ] too [tuː] adv. 太,过于
- [ ] again [əˈgeɪn] adv. 再一次;又一次
- [ ] almost [ˈɔːlməʊst] adv. 几乎;差不多
- [ ] plastic [ˈplæstɪk] n. 塑料 adj. 塑料的
- [ ] metal [ˈmetl] n. 金属

故事导读：
1. 小朋友，你知道在手机发明之前，人们是怎样相互联系的吗？
2. 试着标记出与通信设备相关的单词吧。

IT Changes Our Lives

David is an 11-year-old boy who loves IT (Information Technology) products. Today his mother took him to an exhibition of IT products.

On the ground floor there was a large hall showing the communication tools from past to today. When they came into the hall, a video on a big screen was showing the way people communicated in the past. People wrote letters to express their feelings of missing friends or family members. Then they needed to go to the post office and put a stamp to make sure letters could be mailed. Later, email appeared. People could send and receive emails easily online. It really saved people a lot of time.

They kept walking along and saw a video showing the functions of the mobile phone. The mobile phone is also called the smartphone or cell phone and can be used everywhere in our daily life. People use it to have video chats with friends and family members miles away. Distance is not a problem anymore on the Internet. With the wide coverage of wifi, it is possible for people to know news in the web page and use various apps for shopping in their spare time.

On the first floor they learned about the development history of players. The players, for example, CD players, DVD players and MP3 players, changed the ways people listen to music. David even tried turning on a radio with a battery.

Later, they also went over other products like electric lights and electric cars.

"These great inventions are the signs of every age. I'll remember them. I hope I can be an inventor to **invent** something **useful** for people in the future!" said David excitedly.

"I am **ready** to see your great inventions," replied David's mother with a smile.

信息技术改变我们的生活

参考译文

大卫是一个喜欢科技产品的11岁男孩。今天，他妈妈带他参观了一场科技产品的展览会。

一楼有一个大厅，展示着从过去到现在的通信工具。他们进入时，一个大屏幕上的视频正在展示人们过去的交流方式。人们通过写信来表达他们对朋友及家人的思念之情。然后他们要去邮局，贴上一张邮票以确保信件能被邮寄出去。之后，电子邮件出现了。人们可以在网上轻松地收发电子邮件。这确实可以让人们节省很多时间。

他们继续往前走，看到了展示手机功能的视频。手机也被称为智能手机或移动电话，在我们的日常生活中无处不在。人们用它与数英里之外的朋友和家人视频聊天。在互联网上，距离不再是问题。随着无线网络的广泛覆盖，人们可以通过网页了解新闻，在闲暇时间使用各种应用软件购物。

在二楼，他们了解了播放器的发展历程。播放器，例如CD播放器、DVD播放器和MP3播放器，改变了人们听音乐的方式。大卫甚至还试着打开了一部装有电池的收音机。

之后，他们还看了其他产品，如电灯、电动汽车等。

"这些伟大的发明是每个时代的标志。我会记住它们的。我希望未来我能成为一个发明家，为人们发明一些有用的东西！" 大卫激动地说。

"我已经准备好看你的伟大发明了。" 大卫的妈妈微笑着回答道。

IT 信息技术
全称 Information Technology 信息技术

video [ˈvɪdiəʊ] *n.* 录像；录影
搭配 a home video 家庭录像

screen [skriːn] *n.* 屏幕；荧光屏
搭配 a computer screen 电脑屏幕

people [ˈpiːpl] *n.* 人们
例句 There were a lot of people at the party. 有许多人参加了聚会。

letter [ˈletə(r)] *n.* 信
搭配 a thank-you letter 感谢信

post [pəʊst] *n.* 邮递；邮寄
搭配 by post 邮寄

office [ˈɒfɪs] *n.* 办公室
搭配 post office 邮局

make sure（**that**）确保

例句 Just make sure that you turn off the light before leaving. 确保你离开之前关灯。

mail [meɪl] v. 邮寄
例句 Don't forget to mail your mother that letter. 别忘了把那封信寄给你妈妈。

email [ˈiːmeɪl] n. 电子邮件

send [send] v. 邮寄；发送
搭配 send a letter 寄信

online [ˌɒnˈlaɪn] adj. 在线的 adv. 在线地

save [seɪv] v. 节省；节约
例句 We should try to save water. 我们应设法节约用水。

mobile [ˈməʊbaɪl] adj. 非固定的；可移动的
搭配 mobile phone 移动电话；手机

smartphone [ˈsmɑːtfəʊn] n. 智能手机
助记 smart（智能的）+phone（电话）

cell phone 移动电话；手机

use [juːz] v. 使用；利用（过去式/过去分词 used）
例句 Can I use your phone? 我可以用一下你的手机吗？

everywhere [ˈevriweə(r)] adv. 处处；到处
助记 every（每个）+where（在哪里）

daily [ˈdeɪli] adj. 每日的；日常的
搭配 the Daily News《每日新闻报》

mile [maɪl] n. 英里

anymore [ˈenimɔː] adv. 再
例句 I won't trust him anymore. 我不再相信他了。

Internet [ˈɪntənet] n. 互联网；因特网

wide [waɪd] adj. 广泛的；范围大的

wifi [ˈwaɪ faɪ] n. 无线网络

possible [ˈpɒsəbl] adj. 可能的；能做到的

例句 Everything is possible. 一切皆有可能。

web [web] n. 网

various [ˈveəriəs] adj. 各种不同的；各种各样的
例句 These tents come in various shapes and sizes. 这些帐篷形状大小各异。

app [æp] n. 应用软件

spare [speə(r)] adj. 空闲的；空余的
搭配 spare time 空闲时间

player [ˈpleɪə(r)] n. 播放器

CD player 激光唱片；光盘播放器

DVD player 数字光碟；DVD 播放器

MP3 player MP3 播放器

even [ˈiːvn] adv. 甚至

turn on 打开
反义 turn off 关上
例句 I want to turn on the radio. 我想打开收音机。

radio [ˈreɪdiəʊ] n. 收音机；无线电广播

battery [ˈbætəri] n. 电池

electric [ɪˈlektrɪk] adj. 电的；用电的
搭配 electric lights 电灯

sign [saɪn] n. 标志；符号
搭配 a road sign 道路标志

remember [rɪˈmembə(r)] v. 记得；记起
例句 I don't remember my first day at school. 我忘了第一天上学的情景。

invent [ɪnˈvent] v. 发明；创造
联想 invention n. 发明；发明物
inventor n. 发明者；发明家
例句 He invented the first electric clock. 他发明了第一个电子闹钟。

useful [ˈjuːsfl] *adj.* 有用的；有益的
搭配 be useful for 对……有用

ready [ˈredi] *adj.* 准备好的

例句 I'm just getting the kids ready for school. 我正在让孩子们为上学做准备。

Exercise

I. Listen and read the phrases aloud.

1. send a letter by post
2. on the Internet
3. listen to a radio
4. turn on and turn off
5. in one's spare time
6. use various apps in our daily life
7. save somebody a lot of time
8. send and receive emails online
9. be ready to do something
10. invent something useful for people

II. Match the words with pictures.

Group 1

1.   A. smartphone
2.   B. radio
3.   C. video
4.   D. letter
5.   E. email

Group 2

1.   A. app
2.   B. screen
3.   C. battery
4.   D. post office
5.   E. Internet

Ⅲ. Listen and choose the correct answer for each question.

1. Where is Judy now?
   A. In the post office.　　B. At an exhibition.　　C. In a bookstore.
2. What did the girl receive as a birthday present last year?
   A. A book.　　B. A smartphone.　　C. A toy.
3. How will Peter tell the girl the details about the party?
   A. By letter.　　B. By phone.　　C. By email.

Ⅳ. Answer the questions.

1. Are you interested in electronic products?

_____

_____

2. Have you written a letter to your best friend?

_____

_____

3. If you are asked to write a letter to your best friend, what will you write?

_____

_____

故事导读：
1. 小朋友，你知道视频博主需要掌握哪些技能吗？
2. 记得标记出新学到的单词和句式哦。

How to Be a Vlogger?

Bob is a boy **whose** dream is to become a vlogger(视频博主) when he **grows** up. He wants to **make** a **variety** of interesting videos and share them with people on **social media**. His parents support him very much. They bought him a **laptop** and a **printer** to encourage him. They think whether his dream comes **true** or not, preparing to be a vlogger will be an **unusual** experience in his life.

Bob got up early on Sunday to record a video. He put the **memory card** into his **digital** camera and prepared to **record** his ideas about some **programmes**. He **started** with a self-introduction and discussed some interesting programmes in funny words. After 40 minutes' recording, he pressed the **stop** button and **uploaded** the video to the **computer**.

Bob **downloaded** a **software** to edit the video and add some soft music to it. He didn't **mean** to show off, but to let people who watch his videos be **pleased**. Once he **completed** editing, he **clicked** on the **mouse** and **keyboard** to visit a **website** and logged in to upload.

Possibly nobody would like his video at first. It is **sad**, but Bob knows that being a vlogger is **exactly** what he wants. There is a voice **deep** inside his heart telling him to stick to it.

"Never say never. I don't need to be better **than** others. Don't **forget** that I **just** want to bring joy to people," he said to himself. **Suddenly**, Bob got a like. He was very excited.

怎样成为一名视频博主？

鲍勃是一个小男孩，他希望长大后成为一名视频博主。他想制作各种有趣的视频，在社交媒体上与人们分享。他的父母非常支持他。他们为他购买了笔记本电脑和打印机来鼓励他。他们认为无论他的梦想成真与否，准备成为一名视频博主都将是他一生中不寻常的经历。

鲍勃星期天很早就起床录制视频。他把存储卡放进数码相机，准备记录他对一些节目的想法。他首先做了自我介绍，然后用风趣的语言讨论了一些有趣的节目。录制40分钟后，他按下了"停止"键，将视频上传到了电脑上。

鲍勃下载了一个软件来剪辑视频，并插入了一些轻音乐。他并不想炫耀，而是想让看视频的人心情愉快。视频剪辑完成后，他点击鼠标和键盘访问了一个网站，登录后上传视频。

一开始可能没有人喜欢他的视频。这让人伤心，但鲍勃知道成为一名视频博主正是他想做的。在他的内心深处有一个声音告诉他要坚持下去。

"永远不要放弃。我不需要比别人更好。别忘了我只是想给人们带来欢乐。"他对自己说。突然，鲍勃收到了一个点赞，他兴奋极了。

Word list

whose [huːz] *det. & pron.* （用于疑问句）谁的
例句 Whose house is that? 那是谁的房子？

grow [grəʊ] *v.* 长大；长高
搭配 grow up 长大

make [meɪk] *v.* 制作；使（过去式/过去分词 made）
搭配 make bread 制作面包

variety [vəˈraɪəti] *n.* 不同种类，多种式样
搭配 a variety of 多种多样的

social media 社交媒体

laptop [ˈlæptɒp] *n.* 笔记本电脑

printer [ˈprɪntə(r)] *n.* 打印机
例句 There's something wrong with the printer. 这台打印机出了故障。

true [truː] *adj.* 真实的

搭配 come true 实现；成真

unusual [ʌnˈjuːʒuəl] *adj.* 独特的；与众不同的
助记 un-（不）+（usual）平常的

memory card 内存卡，存储卡

digital [ˈdɪdʒɪtl] *adj.* 数码的；数字式的
搭配 a digital camera 数码相机

record [rɪˈkɔːd] *v.* 录制；记录
例句 Did you remember to record that programme for me? 你记得为我录下那个节目了吗？

programme [ˈprəʊɡræm] *n.* 节目；计划
搭配 a news programme 新闻节目

start [stɑːt] *v.* 开始，着手
例句 It started to rain. 开始下雨了。

读故事 巧记 KET 核心词汇

stop [stɒp] v. 停止，停下
例句 The car stopped at the traffic lights. 汽车在交通信号灯前停了下来。

upload [ˌʌp'ləʊd] v. 上传
助记 up（向上）+load（装入）

computer [kəm'pju:tə(r)] n. 计算机；电脑
搭配 a personal computer（=PC）个人电脑

download [ˌdaʊn'ləʊd] v. 下载
助记 down（向下）+load（负载）
例句 You can upload or download it. 你可以上传或者下载它。

software ['sɒftweə(r)] n. 软件
搭配 design software 设计软件
助记 soft（软的）+ware（物品）

mean [mi:n] v. 意思是；本意是
例句 What do you mean? 你是什么意思？

pleased [pli:zd] adj. 高兴的；愉快的
例句 I'm pleased to hear about your news. 听到你的消息我很高兴。

complete [kəm'pli:t] v. 完成；结束
例句 The project should be completed within a year. 这项工程必须在一年之内完成。

click [klɪk] v. 点击，单击
例句 Click the OK button to start. 点击"确认"键启动。

mouse [maʊs] n. 鼠标；老鼠
搭配 click the mouse 点击鼠标

keyboard ['ki:bɔ:d] n. 键盘

助记 key（键）+board（板）

website ['websaɪt] n. 网站
助记 web（网）+site（站点）
搭配 visit the website 访问网站

possibly ['pɒsəbli] adv. 可能；或许
例句 I can't possibly answer that question. 我不可能回答那个问题。

nobody ['nəʊbədi] pron. 没有人；没有任何人
助记 no（没有）+body（身体）

sad [sæd] adj. 难过的；令人难过的
例句 I was sad that she had to go. 她得走了，我对此很难过。

exactly [ɪg'zæktli] adv. 准确地；确切地
例句 Your answer is exactly right. 你的回答完全正确。

deep [di:p] adj. 深的；厚的 adv. 深深地；在深处
搭配 a deep river 很深的河

than [ðən] prep. 比
例句 I'm older than her. 我比她年龄大。

forget [fə'get] v. 忘记（过去式 forgot；过去分词 forgotten）
反义 remember 记得
例句 I never forget a face. 见过的面孔我从不忘记。

just [dʒʌst] adv. 只不过；正好

suddenly ['sʌdənli] adv. 突然；忽然
例句 "Listen!" said Doyle suddenly. "你听！"多伊尔突然说道。

Day 18

Exercise

I. Listen and read the phrases aloud.

1. grow up
2. computer and laptop
3. mouse and keyboard
4. upload and download
5. start and stop
6. sad and pleased
7. a digital camera
8. a variety of software
9. click on the website
10. record and make videos

II. Label the pictures.

1. c_ _ _ _ _ _ _   4. p_ _ _ _ _ _   5. m_ _ _ _ _ c_ _ _
2. m_ _ _ _
3. k_ _ _ _ _ _ _

6. l_ _ _ _ _   7. v_ _ _ _   8. d_ _ _ _ _ _ c_ _ _ _ _

III. Listen and choose the correct answer for each question.

1. Whose videos has the girl watched recently?
   A. Science Tom.   B. Science Penny.   C. Science Leo.
2. Which part of the girl's computer doesn't work?
   A. The printer.   B. The mouse.   C. The keyboard.
3. What will the boy share in his videos?
   A. Piano lessons.   B. Learning methods.   C. Funny jokes.

109

IV. **Read the email from your English friend, Jackson.**

From:	Jackson
To:	

Hi! Last Saturday my parents bought me a laptop as a gift. Do you have a computer or laptop? What do you use it for? Do you know how to upload something to it? Let me know.

Write an email to Jackson and answer the questions.

Write **25 words** or more.

Unit 10
Time, Colour, Weather and Nature

Pre-test

快速浏览下面的单词，自测一下，看看你是否已经掌握了呢？记得标记你不熟悉的单词，多多复习哦！

- [ ] first [fɜːst] adv. 第一；首先 adj. 第一的
- [ ] second ['sekənd] adv. 第二 adj. 第二的 n. 秒
- [ ] ice [aɪs] n. 冰
- [ ] storm [stɔːm] n. 暴风雨
- [ ] black [blæk] adj. 黑的；黑色的
- [ ] pale [peɪl] adj. 苍白的；浅色的
- [ ] grey [ɡreɪ] adj. 灰色的（英式）
- [ ] gray [ɡreɪ] adj. 灰色的（美式）
- [ ] pink [pɪŋk] adj. 粉红色的
- [ ] good morning 早上好；上午好
- [ ] good afternoon 下午好
- [ ] good evening 晚上好
- [ ] good night 晚上好
- [ ] white [waɪt] adj. 白的；白色的
- [ ] purple ['pɜːpl] adj. 紫色的
- [ ] air [eə(r)] n. 空气
- [ ] fire ['faɪə(r)] n. 火
- [ ] plant [plɑːnt] n. 植物
- [ ] hill [hɪl] n. 山丘；小山
- [ ] river ['rɪvə(r)] n. 河；江
- [ ] wood [wʊd] n. 木材；树林
- [ ] begin [bɪ'ɡɪn] v. 开始；启动
- [ ] rainforest ['reɪnfɒrɪst] n. （热带）雨林

故事导读：

1. 小朋友，你知道怎样描述天气吗？来看看北京一年四季的天气吧。
2. 试着标出文中描述天气的单词吧。

The Weather in Beijing

Beijing is in the northeast of China and has been the capital of the country for over eight centuries. It attracts millions of tourists from all over the world every year. If you're looking at the calendar and planning for a trip, please notice the weather in Beijing.

Beijing has four distinct seasons: short windy spring, hot and wet summer, cool and pleasant autumn, and long chilly winter. The sun in Beijing shines quite often all year round.

Here are the monthly temperatures:

Month Temperature	January	February	March	April	May	June	July	August	September	October	November	December
Minimum (℃)	−8	−6	0	8	14	19	22	21	15	8	0	−6
Maximum (℃)	2	5	12	20	26	30	31	30	26	19	10	4

In spring, the temperature increases rapidly and the weather becomes warm. Sometimes the city can be covered by yellow dust which comes from the deserts of Mongolia(蒙古).

It's already as hot as in the middle of summer from the beginning of June and it often rains. Short and heavy thunderstorms may come suddenly in the afternoon on sunny days.

It becomes pleasant in autumn. It is the best time to visit the city, especially in September and October. The green leaves on the trees turn red, golden and brown and the colour of the sky is usually bright blue.

In winter, the temperature sometimes can drop to -15℃ at midnight. Cold winds blow from the north. Although winter is a dry season, sometimes it snows. Don't be worried that it gets dark too early—many celebrations take place at night during the Spring Festival holiday, which is usually in January or February.

北京的天气

参考译文

北京位于中国的东北部，建都史已有 800 多年。它每年都吸引着来自世界各地的成千上万的游客。如果你正在翻阅日历并计划着下一次旅行，请注意一下北京的天气。

北京四季分明：短暂而多风的春季，炎热而潮湿多雨的夏季，凉爽宜人的秋季，以及漫长寒冷的冬季。北京基本上一整年都有太阳照耀。

下面是每个月的气温表：

月份 温度	一月	二月	三月	四月	五月	六月	七月	八月	九月	十月	十一月	十二月
最低（℃）	-8	-6	0	8	14	19	22	21	15	8	0	-6
最高（℃）	2	5	12	20	26	30	31	30	26	19	10	4

春天，气温迅速回升，天气逐渐转暖。有时候这座城市会受到来自蒙古沙漠的黄沙的影响。

北京六月初就已经和盛夏一样炎热了，而且经常下雨。在阳光灿烂的日子里，短暂的暴雨有可能在下午突然到来。

秋天的天气很宜人。这是游览这座城市的最佳时节，特别是在九月和十月。树上的绿叶变成红色、黄色和棕色，天空的颜色通常是明亮的蓝色。

冬天，气温有时会在午夜时分降到零下 15℃。寒冷的风从北面刮来。虽然冬天是一个干燥的季节，但有时也会下雪。不要担心天黑得太早——春节假期期间，通常是一月或者二月，有很多庆祝活动都会在夜晚举办。

for [fɔː(r)] *prep.* 给，对；为了
例句 There's a letter for you. 这儿有你的一封信。

century [ˈsentʃəri] *n.* 世纪；百年
搭配 the 20th century 20 世纪

world [wɜːld] *n.* 世界

搭配 travel all over the world 周游世界

calendar [ˈkælɪndə(r)] *n.* 日历
搭配 a calendar for 2021 2021 年日历

windy [ˈwɪndi] *adj.* 多风的，风大的
搭配 a windy day 大风天

spring [sprɪŋ] *n.* 春天
搭配 next spring 明年春天

hot [hɒt] *adj.* 热的
搭配 a hot dry summer 炎热干燥的夏天

wet [wet] *adj.* 潮湿的
搭配 wet clothes 湿衣服

summer [ˈsʌmə(r)] *n.* 夏天；夏季
搭配 a summer's day 夏日

cool [kuːl] *adj.* 凉爽的
搭配 a cool dry place 干燥凉爽的地方

autumn [ˈɔːtəm] *n.* 秋天
搭配 in early autumn 在初秋

winter [ˈwɪntə(r)] *n.* 冬天；冬季
搭配 last winter 去年冬天

sun [sʌn] *n.* 太阳
例句 The sun is shining and birds are singing. 阳光照耀，鸟儿歌唱。

year [jɪə(r)] *n.* 年
搭配 all year round 全年

monthly [ˈmʌnθli] *adj.* 每月的；每月一次的

month [mʌnθ] *n.* 月；一个月的时间
搭配 several months later 几个月以后

January [ˈdʒænjuəri] *n.* 一月（缩写 Jan.）

February [ˈfebruəri] *n.* 二月（缩写 Feb.）

March [mɑːtʃ] *n.* 三月（缩写 Mar.）

April [ˈeɪprəl] *n.* 四月（缩写 Apr.）

May [meɪ] *n.* 五月

June [dʒuːn] *n.* 六月（缩写 Jun.）

July [dʒuˈlaɪ] *n.* 七月（缩写 Jul.）

August [ˈɔːgəst] *n.* 八月（缩写 Aug.）

September [sepˈtembə(r)] *n.* 九月（缩写 Sept.）

October [ɒkˈtəʊbə(r)] *n.* 十月（缩写 Oct.）

November [nəʊˈvembə(r)] *n.* 十一月（缩写 Nov.）

December [dɪˈsembə(r)] *n.* 十二月（缩写 Dec.）

weather [ˈweðə(r)] *n.* 天气
例句 Did you have good weather on your trip? 你旅途中天气好吗？

warm [wɔːm] *adj.* 温暖的
搭配 a warm September evening 9月的一个温暖夜晚

yellow [ˈjeləʊ] *adj.* 黄色的 *n.* 黄色
搭配 pale yellow flowers 淡黄色的花朵

desert [ˈdezət] *n.* 沙漠；荒原
搭配 the Sahara Desert 撒哈拉大沙漠

beginning [bɪˈgɪnɪŋ] *n.* 开头；开始部分
搭配 at the beginning of July 七月初

rain [reɪn] *n.* 雨 *v.* 下雨
例句 The rain poured down. 雨瓢泼而下。

thunderstorm [ˈθʌndəstɔːm] *n.* 雷雨
助记 thunder（雷）+ storm（暴风雨）
例句 She got caught in a thunderstorm. 她遇上了雷雨。

afternoon [ˌɑːftəˈnuːn] *n.* 午后，下午
搭配 in the afternoon 在下午
助记 after（在……之后）+ noon（正午）

sunny [ˈsʌni] *adj.* 阳光充足的
搭配 a sunny day 阳光明媚的日子

especially [ɪˈspeʃəli] *adv.* 尤其；特别
例句 I love Rome, especially in the spring.

我喜爱罗马，尤其是春天的罗马。

green [griːn] *adj.* 绿色的 *n.* 绿色
搭配 green fields 绿油油的农田

tree [triː] *n.* 树
搭配 plant a tree 植树

red [red] *adj.* 红色的
搭配 a red car 红色的汽车

golden ['gəʊldən] *adj.* 金色的；金黄色的
搭配 golden hair 金发

brown [braʊn] *adj.* 棕色的；褐色的
搭配 brown eyes 褐色的眼睛

colour ['kʌlə(r)] *n.* 颜色
搭配 the colour of the sky 天空的颜色

sky [skaɪ] *n.* 天空
搭配 the night sky 夜空

bright [braɪt] *adj.* 明亮的；鲜艳的
例句 I like bright colours. 我喜欢明亮的色彩。

blue [bluː] *adj.* 蓝色的
搭配 a blue shirt 蓝色的衬衫

midnight ['mɪdnaɪt] *n.* 午夜；半夜12点钟

助记 mid-（中间的）+ night（夜晚）
例句 They had to leave at midnight. 他们不得不半夜离开。

wind [wɪnd] *n.* 风
搭配 strong winds 大风

dry [draɪ] *adj.* 干的；干燥的
搭配 the dry season 旱季

snow [snəʊ] *n.* 雪 *v.* 下雪
例句 Snow is falling heavily. 天正下着大雪。

dark [dɑːk] *adj.* 黑暗的；深色的
例句 What time does it get dark in summer? 夏天什么时候天黑？

night [naɪt] *n.* 夜晚
搭配 at night 在夜晚

during ['djʊərɪŋ] *prep.* 在……期间
搭配 during the day 在白天

festival ['festɪvl] *n.* 节日
搭配 the Spring Festival 春节

holiday ['hɒlədeɪ] *n.* 假期
搭配 the summer holidays 暑假

Exercise

1. Listen and read the phrases aloud.

1. spring, summer, autumn and winter
2. hot and wet
3. sunny and warm
4. cool and dry
5. rainy and windy
6. wind and snow
7. red and blue
8. yellow and green
9. golden and brown
10. blue sky
11. month and year
12. festival and holiday

II. Label the pictures.

Season: 1. s_ _ _ _ _
Months: March, April, May
Weather: 2. w_ _ _ _ and warm
Colour: green

Season: summer
Months: 3. J_ _ _, July, August
Weather: 4. h_ _ and 5. r_ _ _ _
Colour: blue

Season: 6. a_ _ _ _ _
Months: September, October, November
Weather: 7. c_ _ _ and pleasant
Colour: 8. r_ _ and golden

Season: 9. w_ _ _ _ _
Months: December, 10. J_ _ _ _ _ _, February
Weather: chilly and snowy
Colour: white

III. Listen and choose the correct answer for each question.

1. What is the weather like in winter in London?
   A. Cool and pleasant.　　B. Cold and rainy.　　C. Cold and dry.
2. If you're going to London in summer, which is the stuff you don't need to bring with you?
   A. A light jacket.　　B. A thick coat.　　C. An umbrella.

3. What is the rainiest season in London?

   A. Spring.   B. Summer.   C. Autumn.

IV. Answer the questions.

1. Which month were you and your best friend born in?

_____

_____

2. What is your favourite season? Why?

_____

_____

3. Which do you prefer, sunny or rainy weather? Why?

_____

_____

故事导读：
1. 小朋友，来看看这三个好朋友是怎样在群聊中筹备一次大自然之旅的吧。
2. 试着标记出表示星期的单词吧。

Let's Go Camping!

Monday 30 June

Elyse: Good evening! How're you guys doing tonight?

Anna: I'm very good. I just finished my homework.

Bradley: Me too. How about you?

Elyse: I'm checking my weekly schedule…I'm afraid that I can't go on Friday around midday as we planned before. I forgot that day I have to see a doctor in the afternoon. Can we leave on Saturday morning?

Bradley: Is it possible that you'll visit the doctor before that day? The weather forecast shows it will be cloudy and foggy on Saturday. We won't be able to see the beautiful full moon and the stars if we arrive one day later.

Elyse: Maybe visiting a doctor can be on next weekday. I'll confirm it by Wednesday!

Tuesday 1 July

Elyse: I have changed the time to visit the doctor so we can leave at noon on Friday! I will drop by the grocery store on Thursday after class.

Anna: Cool! I'll go with you. I've got everything ready except for the food and drinks.

Bradley: Great! There's still enough space in my backpack so we can get much food.

Sunday 6 July

Anna: The trip was fantastic! Can you guys send pictures of us in the mountain forest and by the Silver Lake? Also the ones on the grass field! I want to share those great moments on my social media.

Bradley: Sure! It must be one of my favourite camping trips. We're so lucky that the

clouds and **fog** were blown away.

Elyse: It's always nice to be in **nature**, especially with you guys! Maybe we should plan an **island** trip next time!

一起去露营吧!

6月30日 星期一

伊利斯：晚上好！你们今天晚上过得怎么样？

安娜：我很好，我刚完成作业。

布拉德利：我也是。你呢？

伊利斯：我正在查看这周的日程表……恐怕我不能像之前计划的那样在周五中午左右出发了。我忘记了那天下午要去看医生。我们可以周六早上出发吗？

布拉德利：你有没有可能在那天之前去看医生呢？天气预报显示周六多云多雾。如果我们晚一天到达，就无法看到漂亮的满月和星星了。

伊利斯：我也许可以下个工作日去看医生。我会在周三之前确定的！

7月1日 星期二

伊利斯：我已经更改了去看医生的时间，所以我们可以在周五中午出发了！周四放学后我会顺路去一趟杂货店。

安娜：太好了！我和你一起去。我已经把所有东西都准备好了，除了吃的和喝的。

布拉德利：太棒了！我的背包有足够的空间，所以我们可以带很多食物。

7月6日 星期日

安娜：这次旅行太棒了！你们可以把我们在山地森林和银湖拍的照片发给我吗？还有在草地上的照片！我想把这些美好的瞬间分享在社交网络上。

布拉德利：好的！这无疑是我最喜欢的一次露营旅行。云层和雾都被吹走了，我们太幸运了。

伊利斯：能够身处自然之中总是很美好，特别是和你们在一起！或许下次我们可以计划一次海岛之旅！

Monday [ˈmʌndeɪ] *n.* 星期一
例句 We'll meet on Monday. 我们星期一见。

evening [ˈiːvnɪŋ] *n.* 晚上；傍晚
搭配 in the evening 在晚上

tonight [təˈnaɪt] *adv.* 在今晚，在今夜
例句 It's very cold tonight. 今天晚上很冷。

weekly [ˈwiːkli] *adj.* 每周的
搭配 weekly meetings 周会

Friday [ˈfraɪdeɪ] *n.* 星期五
搭配 Friday evening 星期五晚上

midday [ˌmɪdˈdeɪ] *n.* 中午，正午
搭配 at midday 在中午

before [bɪˈfɔː(r)] *prep.* 在……之前 *adv.* 以前 *conj.* 在……以前
搭配 the day before yesterday 前天
例句 I think we've met before. 我觉得我们以前见过面。

Saturday [ˈsætədeɪ] *n.* 星期六

morning [ˈmɔːnɪŋ] *n.* 早晨；上午
搭配 in the morning 在早晨

cloudy [ˈklaʊdi] *adj.* 多云的
搭配 a grey, cloudy day 灰暗多云的一天

foggy [ˈfɒgi] *adj.* 有雾的
搭配 a foggy road 雾茫茫的道路

moon [muːn] *n.* 月亮；月球
例句 There's no moon tonight. 今晚看不见月亮。

star [stɑː(r)] *n.* 星；明星
例句 We camped out under the stars. 我们露天宿营。

weekday [ˈwiːkdeɪ] *n.* 工作日
搭配 on a weekday 在工作日

Wednesday [ˈwenzdeɪ] *n.* 星期三

Tuesday [ˈtjuːzdeɪ] *n.* 星期二
例句 Are you busy next Tuesday? 下周二你忙吗？

noon [nuːn] *n.* 中午；正午
搭配 at noon 在中午

Thursday [ˈθɜːzdeɪ] *n.* 星期四

except [ɪkˈsept] *prep.* 除……之外 *conj.* 除了

例句 We work every day except Sunday. 我们除星期天外每天都工作。

space [speɪs] *n.* 空间；太空
搭配 make space for 为……腾地方

Sunday [ˈsʌndeɪ] *n.* 星期日

mountain [ˈmaʊntən] *n.* 高山
搭配 climb a mountain 爬山

forest [ˈfɒrɪst] *n.* 森林
搭配 a forest fire 森林火灾

silver [ˈsɪlvə(r)] *adj.* 银色的 *n.* 银
搭配 silver hair 银发

lake [leɪk] *n.* 湖
例句 We swam in the lake. 我们在湖里游泳。

grass [grɑːs] *n.* 草；草地
搭配 on the grass 在草地上

field [fiːld] *n.* 田地；领域
搭配 a field of wheat 一片麦田

moment [ˈməʊmənt] *n.* 片刻；瞬间
例句 One moment, please. 请稍候。

must [mʌst] *mv.* 必须；一定
例句 I'm sorry, but I must go now. 对不起，但是我得马上走。

cloud [klaʊd] *n.* 云；云朵
例句 The sun went behind a cloud. 太阳躲在了一朵云的后面。

fog [fɒg] *n.* 雾
例句 The fog finally lifted. 雾终于散了。

nature [ˈneɪtʃə(r)] *n.* 自然
搭配 the beauties of nature 自然界中美好的事物

island [ˈaɪlənd] *n.* 岛

Exercise

I. Listen and read the phrases aloud.

1. morning and evening
2. midday and midnight
3. fog and cloud
4. foggy and cloudy
5. moon and star
6. grass field and mountain forest
7. river and lake
8. Monday and Tuesday
9. Wednesday and Thursday
10. Friday, Saturday and Sunday

II. Label the pictures.

1. m _ _ _   2. s _ _ _   3. m _ _ _ _ _ _ _   4. g _ _ _ _

5. l _ _ _   6. c _ _ _ _   7. i _ _ _ _ _   8. f _ _ _ _ _

III. Listen and choose the correct answer for each question.

1. On what day will Jared go to see the doctor?
   A. Tuesday.   B. Wednesday.   C. Thursday.
2. What will the weather be like in the afternoon?
   A. Cloudy.   B. Sunny.   C. Rainy.
3. What is the colour of the woman's purse?
   A. Red.   B. Blue.   C. Black.

IV. You're going to a national park with your family on Saturday. Write an email to invite your English friend, Elena.

In your email:
- ask Elena to come to the national park with you on Saturday
- explain why you would love to go and what you are going to see
- tell Elena what the weather will be like

Write **25 words** or more.

_____

_____

_____

_____

Unit 11
Invitation

Pre-test

快速浏览下面的单词，自测一下，看看你是否已经掌握了呢？记得标记你不熟悉的单词，多多复习哦！

- [ ] now [naʊ] *adv.* 现在；目前
- [ ] number [ˈnʌmbə(r)] *n.* 数字；数量
- [ ] same [seɪm] *adj.* 相同的 *pron.* 相同的事物
- [ ] hate [heɪt] *v.* 厌恶，讨厌
- [ ] belong [bɪˈlɒŋ] *v.* 属于
- [ ] both [bəʊθ] *pron. & det.* 两个，两个都
- [ ] minute [ˈmɪnɪt] *n.* 分钟
- [ ] fine [faɪn] *adj.* 美好的；身体好的
- [ ] part [pɑːt] *n.* 部分
- [ ] able [ˈeɪbl] *adj.* 能；能够；有才能的
- [ ] soft [sɒft] *adj.* 柔软的
- [ ] nice [naɪs] *adj.* 令人愉快的
- [ ] rich [rɪtʃ] *adj.* 富有的
- [ ] carry [ˈkæri] *v.* 拿；提
- [ ] careful [ˈkeəfl] *adj.* 小心的；谨慎的
- [ ] look out 注意；留神
- [ ] get on 上车；继续做
- [ ] get off 下车；离开
- [ ] and [ənd] *conj.* 和；与
- [ ] or [ɔː(r)] *conj.* 或者
- [ ] but [bʌt] *conj.* 但是
- [ ] so [səʊ] *conj.* 因此

故事导读：
1. 小朋友，你喜欢和好朋友一起去看电影吗？
2. 试着圈出可以用来赞美别人的形容词吧。

What Shall We Do This Weekend?

Weekend is coming. Billy had spent a boring week, so he wanted to invite his friend Jack to do something interesting over the weekend. He gave a call to Jack.

"Hi! Jack! It's Billy. Are you doing anything over the weekend? Shall we go out to do something interesting?" asked Billy.

Jack received Billy's phone call happily and said, "Thanks for your invitation! I would prefer to go out than do nothing at home. Do you have any ideas?"

Billy thought for a moment and said, "What about watching a film? There are many new awesome films coming out in the cinema. I can't wait to watch them. Let's go to the cinema tomorrow."

"OK." answered Jack and added, "In addition, perhaps we can go skating after watching a film, I suppose. Skating is wonderful in summertime, right?"

Billy is not good at skating, so he answered, "I really hope that I can enjoy it, but I'm worried about my skills."

"OK, never mind," said Jack and he offered another idea, "Guess what, there will be a popular music party held by a musician at 7 p.m. I suggest going there to enjoy the music after watching a film."

"Oh, that's perfect. But I'm afraid we cannot go back too late." Billy spoke out his worry.

"It won't. Just two hours. We'd better carefully choose our favourite one from different films before going to the cinema," said Jack.

"Alright." Billy is good at riding and he added, "I will pick you up at 3 p.m. with my small scooter. By the way, don't forget to bring an umbrella because it will be rainy tomorrow."

"OK. See you later!" Jack said and hung up the telephone.

这个周末我们做什么呢？

参考译文

周末就要到了。比利度过了无聊的一周，所以他想邀请他的朋友杰克在周末做一些有趣的事情。他给杰克打了个电话。

"嗨！杰克！我是比利。你周末有什么安排吗？我们去做点有趣的事情好吗？"比利问道。

杰克很开心接到比利的电话，他说道："谢谢你的邀请！与在家什么都不做相比，我更愿意出去。你有什么想法吗？"

比利想了想说道："看电影怎么样？电影院有很多精彩的新电影上映。我等不及要看了。我们明天就去吧。"

杰克说："好呀。"他又补充道："另外，也许我们可以看完电影后去滑冰。夏天滑冰很棒，对吗？"

比利不擅长滑冰，所以他回答道："我真希望我能享受滑冰，但我担心我的技术。"

"好吧，没关系。"杰克说。他又给出了一个主意："你猜怎么着，晚上7点有一个音乐家举办的流行音乐派对。我建议看完电影之后去那里欣赏音乐。"

"哦，太好了。但恐怕我们不能回家太晚。"比利说出了他的担忧。

"不会太晚，只需要两个小时。我们最好在去电影院之前从不同的电影中仔细挑选出我们最喜欢的。"杰克说道。

"好的。"比利很擅长骑行，他补充说："我下午3点骑着我的小摩托车来接你。顺便说一声，别忘了带把伞，因为明天会下雨。"

"好的。再见！"杰克说着挂断了电话。

Word list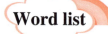

weekend [ˌwiːkˈend] *n.* 周末
助记 week（周）+end（结束）

boring [ˈbɔːrɪŋ] *adj.* 无聊的
搭配 a boring book 无聊的书

week [wiːk] *n.* 星期；一周

want [wɒnt] *v.* 想，想要

注意 want 不用于进行时。

invite [ɪnˈvaɪt] *v.* 邀请
例句 She invited him to her 26th birthday party. 她邀请他参加她的26岁生日聚会。

shall [ʃæl] *mv.* 可以；将要

go out 出去

receive [rɪˈsiːv] *v.* 收到
注意 receive 指客观意义上的收到，比如：receive a letter 收到一封信；accept 强调主观接受，比如：accept one's apology 接受某人的道歉。

invitation [ˌɪnvɪˈteɪʃn] *n.* 邀请
搭配 an invitation to the party 参加晚会的请柬

prefer [prɪˈfɜː(r)] *v.* 更喜欢
搭配 would prefer 宁愿；更喜欢
例句 I would prefer him to be with us next season. 我更希望他在下个赛季和我们在一起。

nothing [ˈnʌθɪŋ] *pron.* 没有什么；无关紧要的事
例句 There is nothing wrong with the car. 那辆车没有任何故障。

idea [aɪˈdɪə] *n.* 想法，主意

what about 怎么样
同义 how about 怎么样

film [fɪlm] *n.* 电影
搭配 watch a film 看电影

new [njuː] *adj.* 新的

awesome [ˈɔːsəm] *adj.* 极好的；令人惊叹的
例句 Wow! That's totally awesome! 哇！真是棒极了！

wait [weɪt] *v.* 等待
例句 Wait for me! 等等我！

tomorrow [təˈmɒrəʊ] *n.* 明天

perhaps [pəˈhæps] *adv.* 也许，或许
例句 Perhaps you are right. 也许你是对的。

suppose [səˈpəʊz] *v.* 认为
例句 Prices will go up, I suppose. 我觉得物价将会上涨。

wonderful [ˈwʌndəfl] *adj.* 极好的

would [wʊd] *mv.* 将会（will 的过去式）；想要
例句 I'd love a coffee. 我想喝杯咖啡。

really [ˈriːəli] *adv.* 真正地，真实地
例句 What do you really think about it? 你到底对这件事怎么看？

hope [həʊp] *v.* 希望
例句 I hope (that) you're okay. 我希望你平安无事。

enjoy [ɪnˈdʒɔɪ] *v.* 享受；喜爱
搭配 enjoy doing sth 喜欢做某事

worried [ˈwʌrid] *adj.* 担心的；担忧的
搭配 be worried about 担心……

mind [maɪnd] *v.* 介意 *n.* 头脑
搭配 never mind 没关系

guess [ges] *v.* 猜测
例句 Guess what? 你猜怎么回事？

popular [ˈpɒpjələ(r)] *adj.* 受欢迎的；流行的

party [ˈpɑːti] *n.* 聚会；派对
搭配 a birthday party 生日聚会

suggest [səˈdʒest] *v.* 建议
搭配 suggest doing sth 建议做某事

perfect [ˈpɜːfɪkt] *adj.* 完美的
例句 Nobody is perfect. 人无完人。

afraid [əˈfreɪd] *adj.* 害怕的，担心的
搭配 be afraid of 害怕；担心

worry [ˈwʌri] *v. & n.* 担心；担忧
例句 Don't worry about me. 别为我担心。

carefully [ˈkeəfəli] *adv.* 仔细地；认真地
联想 careful *adj.* 小心的；谨慎的

different [ˈdɪfrənt] *adj.* 不同的
搭配 be different from 与……不同

读故事 巧记 KET 核心词汇

pick up（开车）接；拾起
例句 I'll pick you up at five. 我5点开车来接你。

scooter ['skuːtə(r)] *n.* 小型摩托车

by the way 顺便说一下

bring [brɪŋ] *v.* 拿来，带来

搭配 bring sth for sb = bring sb sth 给某人带来某物

because [bɪ'kɒz] *conj.* 因为

later ['leɪtə(r)] *adv.* 以后，后来
例句 See you later. 回头见。

Exercise

I. Listen and read the phrases and sentences aloud.

1. invite somebody to watch a film on the weekend
2. pick somebody up with one's scooter
3. receive an invitation
4. would prefer to go out rather than stay at home
5. by the way
6. a perfect idea
7. be afraid of boring things
8. Guess what?
9. Never mind.
10. Tomorrow will be different.

II. Label the pictures.

1. f_ _ _

2. b_ _ _ _ _

3. i_ _ _ _ _ _ _ _ _

4. i_ _ _

5. g_ _ _ _

6. p_ _ _ _

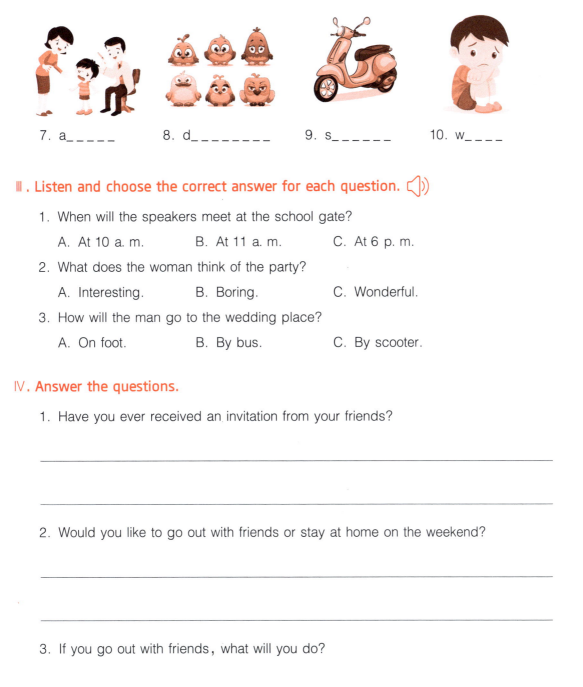

7. a_ _ _ _ _   8. d_ _ _ _ _ _ _ _   9. s_ _ _ _ _ _   10. w_ _ _ _

III. Listen and choose the correct answer for each question.

1. When will the speakers meet at the school gate?
   A. At 10 a. m.   B. At 11 a. m.   C. At 6 p. m.
2. What does the woman think of the party?
   A. Interesting.   B. Boring.   C. Wonderful.
3. How will the man go to the wedding place?
   A. On foot.   B. By bus.   C. By scooter.

IV. Answer the questions.

1. Have you ever received an invitation from your friends?

   _____

   _____

2. Would you like to go out with friends or stay at home on the weekend?

   _____

   _____

3. If you go out with friends, what will you do?

   _____

   _____

故事导读：
1. 小朋友，继续看看Billy和Jack去看电影时的情形吧。
2. 试着圈出你最喜欢的电影类型吧。

Why Not Choose This Film?

When Billy and Jack came to the cinema, they still discussed the films they would watch. Billy likes science fiction films, while Jack likes exciting films. So it's rather difficult to decide which film to watch. There were many kinds of films listed on the screen: romantic stories, comedies, horror films, science fiction films and so on.

Jack was looking for a horror film and he found a great one. He said to Billy, "Why not choose this? I'm crazy about this scary film and I wish you could be my partner to watch it."

Billy looked so scared and said immediately, "Of course not! I cannot accept it. It's terrible. Look at that notice: The film will drive you mad!"

Jack gave up his idea and said, "Oh, sorry. I guess you must like the only science fiction film on the list. Let's choose this one."

"Alright. Let's buy tickets," said Billy with a smile.

(After watching the film...)

"What do you think of the film, Billy?" asked Jack.

"It must be the best science fiction film I've ever seen. The plots are amazing and the background music is pleasant to the ear," answered Billy with joy. Then he added, "What about you?"

However, Jack had different opinions and said, "I am not sure. It's not awful but a little strange. Plus, I am angry about the way people treat the aliens from outer space. I just wanted to take a break during the film."

"What a pity! Although we have different opinions about the film, I still want to make a date with you to watch the next film."

"Oh, I'm very glad to join your next plan," said Jack.

为什么不选这部电影呢？

参考译文　　当比利和杰克来到电影院时，他们还在讨论着即将看的电影。比利喜欢科幻电影，而杰克喜欢刺激的电影。所以，他们很难决定看哪部电影。屏幕上列着多种类型的电影：爱情片、喜剧片、恐怖片、科幻片等。

杰克在找恐怖电影，他发现了一部很不错的影片。他对比利说："我们为什么不选择这部呢？我很喜欢恐怖片，我希望你能陪我一起看。"

比利看起来很害怕，他立即回答说："当然不行！我接受不了。这部电影很可怕。你看那则通告：这部电影会让你发疯！"

杰克放弃了他的想法，说道："哦，对不起。我猜你一定喜欢影片清单上唯一的科幻电影。我们就选这部吧。"

"好的，我们去买票吧。"比利笑着说。

（观看电影后……）

"比利，你觉得这部电影怎么样？"杰克问道。

"这一定是我看过的最棒的科幻电影。故事情节很精彩，背景音乐也很好听。"比利开心地回答道。他随后问道："你觉得怎么样？"

然而，杰克有着不同的看法，他说："我不确定。这部影片并不糟糕，只是有点奇怪。另外，人类对待来自外太空的外星人的方式让我感到很生气。看电影的时候我就想休息一下。"

"真遗憾！虽然我们对电影有着不同的看法，但我还是想约你一起看下一部电影。"

"哦，我非常高兴加入你的下一个观影计划，"杰克说道。

rather [ˈrɑːðə(r)] *adv.* 相当；有点儿
例句 He looks rather like his father. 他看上去很像他的父亲。

difficult [ˈdɪfɪkəlt] *adj.* 困难的
反义 easy 容易的

kind [kaɪnd] *n.* 种类
例句 What kind of house do you live in? 你住的是哪种房子？

look for 寻找

horror [ˈhɒrə(r)] *n.* 恐怖故事（或电影等）；

恐惧

搭配 a horror film 恐怖片

why [waɪ] *adv.* 为什么，为何

搭配 why don't we... = why not... 为什么不……

例句 Why don't we go together? 我们为什么不一起去呢？

crazy [ˈkreɪzi] *adj.* 热衷的；狂热的

搭配 be crazy about 热衷于

scary [ˈskeəri] *adj.* 可怕的，吓人的

搭配 a scary movie 恐怖电影

wish [wɪʃ] *v.* 希望

例句 —Where is he now? ——他现在在哪儿？
—I only wish I knew! ——我要是知道就好了！

partner [ˈpɑːtnə(r)] *n.* 伙伴；搭档

搭配 a dancing partner 舞伴

look [lʊk] *v.* 看来好像；似乎

例句 You look happy. 你看起来很开心。

scared [skeəd] *adj.* 害怕的，受惊的

搭配 be scared of 害怕……

immediately [ɪˈmiːdiətli] *adv.* 立刻地

例句 She answered almost immediately. 她几乎立刻就回答了。

of course（not） 当然（不）

accept [əkˈsept] *v.* 接受；同意

例句 He didn't accept the job. 他不接受那项工作。

terrible [ˈterəbl] *adj.* 可怕的；糟糕的

例句 What terrible news! 多么骇人听闻的消息！

notice [ˈnəʊtɪs] *n.* 通知，公告

例句 They pinned a notice to the door. 他们把通知钉在门上。

mad [mæd] *adj.* 疯的；生气的

例句 I'll go mad if I have to wait much longer. 如果还要等更久的话，我会发疯的。

sorry [ˈsɒri] *adj.* 抱歉的；遗憾的

only [ˈəʊnli] *adj.* 仅有的 *adv.* 只有，仅仅

例句 She's their only daughter. 她是他们的独生女。

alright [ɔːlˈraɪt] *adv.* 好吧

同义 all right 好吧

ticket [ˈtɪkɪt] *n.* 票；入场券

搭配 a plane ticket 机票

think [θɪŋk] *v.* 想；认为

搭配 think of 想起

best [best] *adj.* 最好的

注意 best 是 good 与 well 的最高级形式。

amazing [əˈmeɪzɪŋ] *adj.* 令人惊奇的

例句 That's amazing, isn't it? 真是令人惊叹，是不是？

pleasant [ˈpleznt] *adj.* 令人愉快的

搭配 a pleasant evening 令人愉快的夜晚

however [haʊˈevə(r)] *adv.* 然而

sure [ʃʊə(r)] *adj.* 确定的

例句 I'm not a hundred per cent sure. 我不能百分百肯定。

awful [ˈɔːfl] *adj.* 糟糕的；极讨厌的

例句 It's awful, isn't it? 糟糕透了，不是吗？

strange [streɪndʒ] *adj.* 奇怪的；陌生的

例句 There is something strange about her eyes. 她的眼睛有些异常。

plus [plʌs] *prep.* 和；也；外加

angry [ˈæŋgri] *adj.* 愤怒的；生气的

例句 Are you angry with me for some reason?

Day 22

你是出于某种原因生我的气了吗？

way [weɪ] *n.* 方式；道路
搭配 in this way 用这种方法

break [breɪk] *n.* 间断；休息
搭配 take a break 休息一下

pity ['pɪti] *n.* 遗憾；同情
例句 What a pity! 太遗憾了！

although [ɔːl'ðəʊ] *conj.* 尽管，虽然
注意 although 和 but 不能同时出现在一个句子中。

date [deɪt] *n.* 日期；约见时间

例句 I have a date with Bob. 我和鲍勃有个约会。

glad [glæd] *adj.* 高兴的；乐意的
例句 I'm glad (that) you're feeling better. 我很高兴你感觉好些了。

join [dʒɔɪn] *v.* 参加；加入……之中
例句 Will you join us for lunch? 和我们一起吃午饭好吗？

plan [plæn] *n. & v.* 计划；精心安排
搭配 a three-year plan 三年计划

Exercise

Ⅰ. Listen and read the phrases and sentences aloud.

1. look for a horror film
2. look at that notice
3. Why don't we…?
4. be crazy about
5. take a break
6. amazing and pleasant
7. strange and awful
8. plan to buy a ticket
9. take a break
10. What a pity!

Ⅱ. Match the words with their Chinese meanings.

Group 1

1. difficult   A. 狂热的
2. strange   B. 伙伴
3. horror   C. 困难的
4. crazy   D. 奇怪的
5. partner   E. 恐怖故事

Group 2

1. terrible   A. 令人愉快的
2. pleasant   B. 令人惊奇的
3. amazing   C. 生气的
4. accept   D. 可怕的
5. angry   E. 接受

Ⅲ. Listen and choose the correct answer for each question.

1. What does the woman think of the concert?
   A. Awesome.   B. Awful.   C. Boring.

2. Where will the speakers go next Saturday?

   A. To a cinema.　　　B. To a theatre.　　　C. To a park.

3. What's the relationship between the speakers?

   A. Father and daughter.　B. Brother and sister.　C. Husband and wife.

IV. **Look at the three pictures.**

Write the story shown in the pictures.

Write **35 words** or more.

_____

_____

_____

_____

Unit 12
Health, Medicine and Exercise

Pre-test

快速浏览下面的单词，自测一下，看看你是否已经掌握了呢？记得标记你不熟悉的单词，多多复习哦！

- ☐ baby ['beɪbi] *n.* 婴儿
- ☐ pharmacy ['fɑːməsi] *n.* 药房；药店（美式）
- ☐ ear [ɪə(r)] *n.* 耳朵
- ☐ sick [sɪk] *adj.* 生病的
- ☐ eye [aɪ] *n.* 眼睛
- ☐ dead [ded] *adj.* 死的；失去生命的
- ☐ down [daʊn] *adv. & prep.* 向下；朝下
- ☐ lie down 躺下
- ☐ finger ['fɪŋɡə(r)] *n.* 手指
- ☐ nose [nəʊz] *n.* 鼻子
- ☐ less [les] *det.* 较少的，更少的 *pron.* 较少，更少
- ☐ let [let] *v.* 允许；让
- ☐ like [laɪk] *adv.* 可能 *prep.* 像 *v.* 喜欢
- ☐ someone ['sʌmwʌn] *pron.* 某人
- ☐ somebody ['sʌmbədi] *pron.* 某人
- ☐ including [ɪn'kluːdɪŋ] *prep.* 包括
- ☐ thing [θɪŋ] *n.* 东西；物

故事导读：
1. 小朋友，试着弄清楚 Denis 伤在了哪里吧。
2. 试着把看医生时使用的词圈起来哦。

It Really Hurts!

An ambulance arrived at the health centre. Denis' parents and nurses carried him out of the ambulance.

"Doctor, please save my boy. He's in danger now!" His mum cried.

"What's the problem? Could you tell me what happened to your son? Is it an accident or something happened inside his body?"

"He first went to the gym and then played football with his friends outdoors. He was hit badly by the flying football and fell down crying 'I have a horrible stomach ache!'"

"OK, I see. First of all, I'll do some body check. Body temperature is normal. Brain and neck are fine. There's no obvious blood in the stomach. I think the strong hit caused his stomach a lot of pain. I'll give him a prescription(处方). You take him the tablets from the chemist's to relieve his pain and clean the stomach as well. You should make an appointment in two days to see if he needs any other special treatment."

"Thank you so much, Doctor. We'll look after him carefully in the two days." His mum was relieved, and then turned her head to Denis, "Can you hear me, my boy?"

"Yes, Mum." Denis opened his mouth weakly.

"Oh, my boy. You are finally awake," said his mum excitedly and threw her arms around his neck. "We are all frightened and only hope the hit won't be bad for your stomach and you will be healthy."

真的很痛！

一辆救护车来到了健康中心。丹尼斯的父母和护士把他从救护车里抬了出来。

"医生，请您救救我的孩子。他现在很危险！"他妈妈哭喊着。

"怎么回事？你可以告诉我你儿子怎么了吗？是意外事故还是体内出现了病变？"

"他首先去了体育馆，然后和朋友在室外踢足球。他被飞来的足球狠狠击中了，他哭喊着'我肚子好痛'就倒在了地上。"

"好的，我知道了。首先，我要给他做身体检查。体温正常，脑部和颈部正常，腹部没有明显的出血。我认为猛击导致他的腹部出现了剧烈的疼痛。我给他开一个处方。你去药房给他拿一些药片来止痛，同时也清理一下他的胃。你预约一下两天后再次就诊，看看他是否需要其他的特殊治疗。"

"太谢谢你了，医生。我们这两天会好好照顾他的。"妈妈松了一口气，转过头来对丹尼斯说："你能听到吗，孩子？"

"能听到，妈妈。"丹尼斯微弱地张开嘴说道。

"哦，孩子，你终于醒过来了。"他的妈妈兴奋地说道，并张开双臂搂住了他的脖子。"我们都为你担心呢，只希望这次猛击不会伤害你的腹部，你会健健康康的。"

##

hurt [hɜːt] v. 伤害，受伤（过去式/过去分词 hurt）

ambulance [ˈæmbjələns] n. 救护车

health [helθ] n. 健康，卫生
搭配 mental health 心理健康

danger [ˈdeɪndʒə(r)] n. 危险
搭配 in danger 处于危险中
例句 Smoking is a serious danger to health. 吸烟严重危害健康。

cry [kraɪ] v. 哭；喊叫
例句 It's all right. Don't cry. 不要紧，别哭了。

problem [ˈprɒbləm] n. 问题，麻烦
搭配 health problems 健康问题

accident [ˈæksɪdənt] n. 事故；意外
搭配 a car accident 车祸

something [ˈsʌmθɪŋ] pron. 某事，某物
助记 some（某些）+ thing（事物）

body [ˈbɒdi] n. 身体；主体

gym [dʒɪm] n. 健身房；体育馆
注意 gym 是 gymnasium 的缩写形式。

outdoors [ˌaʊtˈdɔːz] adv. 在户外（形容词 outdoor 户外的）
例句 It was warm enough to be outdoors all afternoon. 天气暖洋洋的，整个下午都可以待在户外。

hit [hɪt] v. 击，打；碰撞
例句 I was hit by a falling stone. 我被一块坠

落的石头击中了。

badly ['bædli] *adv.* 严重地；差（比较级 worse；最高级 worst）
搭配 badly hurt 伤害严重
sing badly 唱得不好

fall [fɔːl] *v. & n.* 落下；跌倒（过去式 fell；过去分词 fallen）
搭配 fall down 跌倒；落下

horrible ['hɒrəbl] *adj.* 讨厌的；糟透的
搭配 a horrible man 讨厌的人
例句 The coffee tastes horrible. 这种咖啡难喝极了。

stomach ache 胃痛；腹痛

see [siː] *v.* 看见；理解
例句 —It opens like this. ——这样就打开了。
—Oh, I see. ——哦，我明白了。

first of all 首先

temperature ['temprətʃə(r)] *n.* 温度；体温
搭配 high temperature 高温

brain [breɪn] *n.* 大脑，头脑
搭配 brain storm 头脑风暴

neck [nek] *n.* 脖子

blood [blʌd] *n.* 血
搭配 give blood 献血

stomach ['stʌmək] *n.* 胃；腹部
搭配 stomach pains 肚子疼

pain [peɪn] *n.* 疼痛；痛苦
例句 No pains, no gains. 不劳无获。

tablet ['tæblət] *n.* 药片
近义 pill 药丸；药片
搭配 vitamin tablets 维生素片

chemist's ['kemɪsts] *n.* 药房（英式）
同义 drugstore/pharmacy 药房（美式）

clean [kliːn] *v.* 打扫，使干净 *adj.* 干净的
例句 Have you cleaned your teeth? 你刷过牙了吗？

as well 也，同样
搭配 as well as 和……一样

appointment [ə'pɔɪntmənt] *n.* 预约，约定
搭配 make an appointment 预约

if [ɪf] *conj.* 如果；是否
同义 whether 是否

any ['eni] *det. & pron.* 任何

special ['speʃl] *adj.* 特殊的
例句 She has a special way of smiling. 她微笑的样子有些特别。

look after 照顾
同义 take care of 照顾
例句 I love looking after the children. 我喜欢照顾孩子们。

head [hed] *n.* 头；前端

hear [hɪə(r)] *v.* 听见（过去式/过去分词 heard）

mouth [maʊθ] *n.* 嘴；口

arm [ɑːm] *n.* 手臂；胳膊
搭配 arm in arm 臂挽着臂

frightened ['fraɪtnd] *adj.* 受惊的；害怕的
例句 What are you frightened of? 你怕什么？

bad [bæd] *adj.* 坏的；不善于（比较级 worse；最高级 worst）
搭配 be bad for 对……不利；对……有害
be bad at 不擅长……

healthy ['helθi] *adj.* 健康的，有益健康的
搭配 stay healthy 保持健康

Exercise

I. Listen and read these phrases and sentences aloud.

1. first of all
2. look after
3. make an appointment
4. hear and see
5. No pains, no gains.
6. Her brain was hurt in that accident.
7. Nancy's friend had a horrible stomach ache in the gym.
8. Outdoor temperature fell down last night.
9. These special tablets at the chemist's can't make you healthy.
10. The pain in his head really made him frightened.

II. Label the pictures.

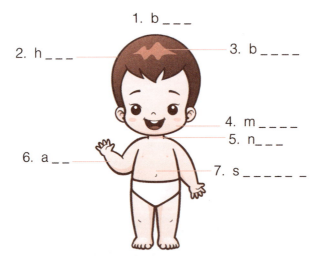

1. b _ _ _
2. h _ _ _
3. b _ _ _ _
4. m _ _ _ _
5. n _ _ _
6. a _ _
7. s _ _ _ _ _ _

III. Listen and then match the body parts and results.

Body Parts	Results
1. mouth ☐	A. normal
2. head ☐	B. badly hurt
3. stomach ☐	C. lightly hurt
	D. hard to say

IV. Answer the questions.

1. Have you ever been ill?

   _____

   _____

2. Do you want to be a doctor in the future? Why/Why not?

   _____

   _____

3. When was the last time you cried?

   _____

   _____

故事导读：
1. 小朋友，圈出文中描述身体部位的单词吧。
2. 试着说说你认为很健康的生活习惯吧。

How to Keep Healthy

Cindy and Lucy are doing some exercise in the gym.

"Today I feel ill and have back pain. I also have strange feelings in my head. I need to rest in that chair." Lucy held her head and seemed very tired.

"Your face looks so white. Are you having a headache? And your legs, your feet, they are not in a good condition, right?" Cindy asked Lucy for more details.

"Exactly! I didn't sleep well last night, and I had a toothache when I brushed my teeth with my toothbrush this morning. When I combed my hair, I felt something strange somewhere in my head," said Lucy weakly.

"Poor you. I'm sure that you have got a cold! You should go to the chemist's to get some medicine."

"Yes. And I think I should do more exercise to keep fit."

"That's right, Lucy. We both should do it. To extend(延长) the length of life and improve the quality of life, we should do some outdoor sports, including jogging and bicycling, and so on. We can also do some indoor sports when we're at home, for example, yoga! Instead of being lazy, we should keep good habits."

"I love yoga, which makes me relaxed from head to toe. In addition, we'd better give up bad habits, like smoking. A lot of people die from smoking every year."

"I totally agree with you. To keep healthy, it's also important to keep ourselves clean by washing our hands with soap when we come back home from outside."

"Yes. Let's keep healthy and live a life of high quality!"

如何保持健康

辛迪和露西在健身房里做运动。

"我今天感觉不舒服，而且背痛，头也有一种奇怪的感觉。我需要坐在那把椅子上休息一下。"露西抱住自己的头，她看起来很累。

"你的脸看起来很苍白。你头疼吗？你的腿和脚是不是都不太对劲？"辛迪想向露西了解更多细节。

"没错！我昨晚没睡好，早晨用牙刷刷牙的时候牙疼，梳头的时候感觉脑袋里有个地方怪怪的。"露西有气无力地说。

"太可怜了，我敢肯定你是感冒了！你应该去药店买些药。"

"是的。我觉得我得加强锻炼来保持健康了。"

"没错，露西。我们都需要加强锻炼。为了延长寿命、提高生活质量，我们应该多做一些户外运动，包括慢跑、骑自行车等。我们也可以在家里做一些室内运动，比如说瑜伽！我们还需要保持良好的生活习惯，而不是犯懒。"

"我喜欢瑜伽，它使我从头到脚都能得到放松。另外，我们应该戒掉像吸烟这样的坏习惯。每年都有很多人因为吸烟而死亡。"

"我完全同意。保持健康还有一个很重要的方式，那就是从户外回到家之后要用肥皂洗手。"

"是的，让我们保持健康，过高品质的生活！"

Word list

do [du] v. 做，干（过去式 did；过去分词 done）
例句 What can I do for you? 我能为您做点什么？

some [sʌm] det. & pron. 一些，若干
例句 Have some more vegetables. 再吃点蔬菜吧。

exercise [ˈeksəsaɪz] n. 运动；练习
搭配 do some exercise 做运动

feel [fiːl] v. 感觉
例句 I feel sorry for him. 我为他感到可惜。

ill [ɪl] adj. 有病的；不舒服的
搭配 seriously ill 病情严重
同义 sick 生病的

back [bæk] n. 背部，背
搭配 back pain 背痛

feeling [ˈfiːlɪŋ] n. 感觉（pl. feelings）
例句 I've got a tight feeling in my stomach. 我觉得胃部胀痛。

hold [həʊld] v. 捂住；拿着（过去式/过去分词 held）
例句 She was holding a large box. 她提着一

只大箱子。

very [ˈveri] *adv.* 很，非常
例句 Thank you very much. 非常感谢。

tired [ˈtaɪəd] *adj.* 疲劳的
搭配 be tired of 厌烦……

face [feɪs] *n.* 脸
搭配 a beautiful face 漂亮的脸

headache [ˈhedeɪk] *n.* 头痛
例句 Red wine gives me a headache. 我喝红酒会头痛。

leg [leg] *n.* 腿
搭配 back legs 后腿

foot [fʊt] *n.* 脚（*pl.* feet）

good [gʊd] *adj.* 好的；优质的（比较级 better；最高级 best）

well [wel] *adv.* 好地；完全地（比较级 better；最高级 best）

toothache [ˈtuːθeɪk] *n.* 牙痛
助记 tooth（牙齿）+ache（疼痛）

tooth [tuːθ] *n.* 牙齿（*pl.* teeth）

with [wɪð] *prep.* 用；有；和
反义 without 不用；没有

toothbrush [ˈtuːθbrʌʃ] *n.* 牙刷
助记 tooth（牙齿）+brush（刷子）

comb [kəʊm] *n.* 梳子 *v.* 梳
注意 comb 词尾的 b 不发音。

hair [heə(r)] *n.* 头发
例句 Don't forget to comb your hair! 别忘了梳一下你的头发！

somewhere [ˈsʌmweə(r)] *adv.* 在某处
助记 some（某些）+where（在哪里）

poor [pɔː(r)] *adj.* 可怜的；贫穷的

反义 rich 富有的

cold [kəʊld] *n.* 感冒 *adj.* 冷的
例句 I've got a cold. 我感冒了。

medicine [ˈmedsn] *n.* 药；医学
例句 Did you take your medicine? 你吃过药了吗？

keep [kiːp] *v.* （使）保持，处于（过去式/过去分词 kept）

fit [fɪt] *adj.* 健康的；恰当的
例句 I joined a gym to get fit. 我去健身房健身。

length [leŋθ] *n.* 长度
例句 The river is 300 miles in length. 这条河长 300 英里。

life [laɪf] *n.* 生命；生活

improve [ɪmˈpruːv] *v.* 提高，改善
搭配 improve health 改善健康

include [ɪnˈkluːd] *v.* 包括

indoor [ˈɪndɔː(r)] *adj.* 室内的（indoors *adv.* 在室内）
助记 in（在……里面）+door（门）
反义 outdoor 室外的

instead [ɪnˈsted] *adv.* 代替，反而
搭配 instead of 不是……而是……

lazy [ˈleɪzi] *adj.* 懒惰的

which [wɪtʃ] *pron. & det.* 哪一个；哪些
例句 Which is better exercise—swimming or tennis? 游泳和网球，哪种运动比较好？

toe [təʊ] *n.* 脚趾
搭配 from head to toe 遍布全身；从头到脚

better [ˈbetə(r)] *adj.* 更好的
搭配 had better（do sth）最好（做某事）

smoke [sməʊk] *v.* 吸烟 *n.* 烟
例句 No smoking! 请勿吸烟！

die [daɪ] v. 死亡，熄灭
搭配 die of cancer 死于癌症

hand [hænd] n. 手

搭配 shake hands 握手

soap [səʊp] n. 肥皂
搭配 soap bubbles 肥皂泡

Exercise

Ⅰ. Listen and read these phrases aloud.

1. legs and feet
2. back pain
3. very tired
4. improve the quality of life
5. from head to toe
6. comb your hair and brush your teeth
7. do some exercise to keep fit
8. get some medicine against toothache and headache
9. die from smoking
10. wash hands with soap

Ⅱ. Label the pictures.

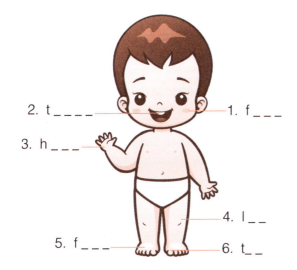

2. t _ _ _ _
3. h _ _ _
5. f _ _ _
1. f _ _ _
4. l _ _
6. t _ _

7. m _ _ _ _ _ _ _

8. s _ _ _ _   9. h _ _ _ _ _ _ _   10. p _ _ _

III. Listen and choose the correct answer for each question.

1. Where are the two speakers?
   A. In a gym.   B. In a swimming pool.   C. On a playground.
2. Which sport doesn't Jenny like?
   A. Swimming.   B. Jogging.   C. Any sports.
3. What does Harry do?
   A. He is a doctor.   B. He is a chemist.   C. He is a fitness trainer.

IV. Look at the three pictures.

Write the story shown in the pictures.

Write **35 words** or more.

_____

_____

_____

_____

Unit 13
Travel and Transport

Pre-test

快速浏览下面的单词，自测一下，看看你是否已经掌握了呢？记得标记你不熟悉的单词，多多复习哦！

- ☐ fly　　　　　　[flaɪ] v. 飞；飞行
- ☐ petrol　　　　　['petrəl] n. 汽油（= gas）
- ☐ helicopter　　　['helɪkɒptə(r)] n. 直升机
- ☐ railway　　　　['reɪlweɪ] n. 铁路；铁道
- ☐ car　　　　　　[kɑː(r)] n. 小汽车；轿车
- ☐ roundabout　　['raʊndəbaʊt] n. （交通）环岛
- ☐ tyre　　　　　　['taɪə(r)] n. 轮胎
- ☐ motorbike　　　['məʊtəbaɪk] n. 轻型摩托车
- ☐ ship　　　　　　[ʃɪp] n. 船 v. 船运；运输
- ☐ visitor　　　　　['vɪzɪtə(r)] n. 参观者；游客
- ☐ move　　　　　[muːv] v. 移动
- ☐ identification　　[aɪ,dentɪfɪ'keɪʃn] n. 确认；身份证明
- ☐ total　　　　　　['təʊtl] adj. 总的；全部的
- ☐ cow　　　　　　[kaʊ] n. 奶牛
- ☐ dinosaur　　　　['daɪnəsɔː(r)] n. 恐龙
- ☐ duck　　　　　　[dʌk] n. 鸭
- ☐ horse　　　　　[hɔːs] n. 马
- ☐ insect　　　　　['ɪnsekt] n. 昆虫
- ☐ sheep　　　　　[ʃiːp] n. 羊；绵羊
- ☐ snake　　　　　[sneɪk] n. 蛇
- ☐ tiger　　　　　　['taɪɡə(r)] n. 老虎
- ☐ monkey　　　　['mʌŋki] n. 猴子
- ☐ lion　　　　　　['laɪən] n. 狮子
- ☐ camel　　　　　['kæml] n. 骆驼
- ☐ bear　　　　　　[beə(r)] n. 熊
- ☐ bird　　　　　　[bɜːd] n. 鸟
- ☐ bee　　　　　　[biː] n. 蜜蜂
- ☐ rabbit　　　　　['ræbɪt] n. 兔子

Day 25

故事导读：
1. 小朋友，你喜欢出门旅游吗？让我们来看看Eric小朋友的旅行日记吧。
2. 遇到不熟悉的单词时记得标记出来哦。

Eric's Travel Journal (1)

15th July 2019

Today is the first day of our yearly family travel. Mum and Dad have started to prepare for the trip since last month and I'm really excited about it. Last night, Mum packed our luggage, and helped my sister Jenny and me with our backpacks.

In the morning, we took a taxi to the airport. The traffic was not bad and we arrived just on time. The staff asked to see our passports and checked in our suitcases. Unfortunately, we were told that our flight was delayed because the engine of the plane needed to be repaired, so we had to wait at the lounge with other passengers for two extra hours. Jenny and I were upset but Mum said, "When life gives you lemons, make lemonade." It cheered us up and we spent the time playing games—that was fun!

The plane finally took off at twelve o'clock and the journey took eight hours. I had a window seat. It was so interesting to see the cities from the sky.

We landed in the afternoon. Everything was fine but we couldn't find our way to the guest-house. Dad encouraged me to go to the tourist information centre and ask for help. I was really nervous but I made it! A nice lady told us that we should take the tram at Platform One.

When we arrived at the guest-house, the receptionist gave us a map and a public transport timetable which included trams, trains, buses and boats. I can't wait to use them for tomorrow's sightseeing!

读故事 巧记KET核心词汇

艾瑞克的旅行日记（一）

2019年7月15日

今天是我们家一年一度的家庭旅行的第一天。爸爸妈妈上个月就开始准备这次旅行了，我也为此感到非常兴奋。昨天晚上，妈妈打包了我们的行李，还帮我和妹妹珍妮整理了双肩包。

早上，我们乘坐出租车去机场。交通状况不错，我们正好准时到达。工作人员让我们出示护照，帮我们托运了行李箱。不幸的是，我们被告知飞机晚点了，因为飞机的引擎需要维修。因此，我们不得不和其他乘客一起在候机室里再等待两个小时。珍妮和我很不开心，但是妈妈说，"当生活给你酸柠檬的时候，你可以把它做成好喝的柠檬汁。"这句话让我们高兴起来，我们利用这段时间玩起了游戏——太有意思了！

最终飞机在12点起飞了，整段旅程一共花了八个小时。我坐在靠窗户的位置。从天空俯瞰城市真是太有趣了。

我们的航班在下午降落。一切都很顺利，只是我们找不到去宾馆的路了。爸爸鼓励我去游客信息咨询中心寻求帮助。我非常紧张，但是我做到了！一位亲切的女士告诉我们应该在一号站台搭乘电车。

当我们到达宾馆的时候，前台接待员给了我们一张地图和一份公共交通时刻表，其中包括电车、火车、公交车和轮船的时刻表。我已经迫不及待要在明天观光时用到它们了！

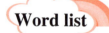

travel ['trævl] *n.* 旅行 *v.* 长途旅行
例句 He travels a lot. 他经常旅行。

trip [trɪp] *n.* （尤指短程往返的）旅行
搭配 a day trip 当天来回的短途旅行

since [sɪns] *prep.* 自……以来
搭配 since then 从那时起

pack [pæk] *v.* 包装；压紧
例句 I packed my luggage by myself. 我自己打包了行李。

luggage ['lʌɡɪdʒ] *n.* 行李；皮箱
搭配 a piece of luggage 一件行李

backpack ['bækpæk] *n.* 双肩背包，背包
助记 back（后背）+pack（背包）

taxi ['tæksi] *n.* 出租车

traffic ['træfɪk] *n.* 交通；运输
搭配 traffic light 红绿灯

arrive [ə'raɪv] *v.* 到达；达成
例句 We arrived at three. 我们三点到的。

passport ['pɑːspɔːt] *n.* 护照，通行证
助记 pass（通过）+port（口岸）

suitcase ['suːtkeɪs] *n.* [旅行用的]手提箱
助记 suit（服装）+case（箱子）

unfortunately [ʌn'fɔːtʃənətli] *adv.* 不幸地
反义 fortunately/luckily 幸运地

delay [dɪ'leɪ] *v.* 延迟；延期 *n.* 延迟的时间
（过去式/过去分词 delayed）

搭配 a delay of two hours 延迟两个小时
例句 The flight is delayed. 航班延误了。

engine [ˈendʒɪn] *n.* 引擎；发动机
搭配 start the engine 发动引擎

plane [pleɪn] *n.* 飞机
同义 aeroplane/airplane 飞机
例句 They arrived in London by plane. 他们乘坐飞机抵达伦敦。

repair [rɪˈpeə(r)] *v.* 修理；修补
搭配 repair a car 修理汽车

passenger [ˈpæsɪndʒə(r)] *n.* 旅客；乘客
搭配 a passenger train 客运列车

upset [ˌʌpˈset] *adj.* 难过的；不高兴的；沮丧的

spend [spend] *v.* 度过，消磨（时光）；花费
例句 Blair has spent lots of money on his hobby. 布莱尔在他的爱好上花了很多钱。

take off 起飞；脱下；离开
例句 The plane took off at night. 飞机在夜里起飞了。

journey [ˈdʒɜːni] *n.* （尤指长途）旅行；行程
例句 Life is a journey. 人生就是一段旅程。

seat [siːt] *n.* 座位
搭配 a window seat 挨窗户的座位
a corner seat 角落里的座位

guest-house [ˈgesthaʊs] *n.* 宾馆；小型家庭旅馆
近义 hotel 旅馆

tourist [ˈtʊərɪst] *n.* 旅游者，观光客
搭配 tourist information centre 游客信息咨询中心

tram [træm] *n.* 有轨电车
同义 streetcar 有轨电车

platform [ˈplætfɔːm] *n.* 平台；月台，站台
例句 What platform does the train go from? 火车从哪个站台发车？

receptionist [rɪˈsepʃənɪst] *n.* 接待员
助记 reception（接待）+-ist（表示"人"）

transport [ˈtrænspɔːt] *n. & v.* 运输；运送
搭配 public transport 公共交通

timetable [ˈtaɪmteɪbl] *n.* 时间表；时刻表；课程表
搭配 school timetable 学校课程表
助记 time（时间）+table（表格）

train [treɪn] *n.* 火车；列车

bus [bʌs] *n.* 公共汽车

boat [bəʊt] *n.* 船

sightseeing [ˈsaɪtsiːɪŋ] *n.* 观光；游览
搭配 go sightseeing 去观光
助记 sight（景象）+see（看）+-ing

Exercise

1. Listen and read the phrases and sentence aloud.

   1. backpack and suitcase
   2. train and tram
   3. bus and boat
   4. yearly family travel
   5. tourist information centre
   6. pack luggage
   7. prepare for the trip
   8. spend time doing something
   9. go sightseeing
   10. Unfortunately, the engine of the plane needs to be repaired.

II. Match the pictures with the words.

Group1

1.   A. tram

2.   B. train

3.   C. bus

4.   D. taxi

5.   E. boat

Group 2

1.   A. timetable

2.   B. passport

3.   C. suitcase

4.   D. receptionist

5.   E. plane

III. Listen and choose the correct answer for each question.

1. How did Richard get to school yesterday?

   A. By bike.   B. By bus.   C. On foot.

2. At which platform should the woman go to catch her train?

   A. Platform 2.   B. Platform 3.   C. Platform 4.

3. How many days did Barb spend in Shanghai?

   A. 2.   B. 3.   C. 4.

IV. **Answer the questions.**

1. How do you get to school every day?
   _____
   _____

2. Do you like travelling?
   _____
   _____

3. Which place is the most interesting during your trip?
   _____
   _____

故事导读：
1. 小朋友，你想知道 Eric 一家还去了哪些地方吗？一起来看看吧。
2. 记得把不熟悉的单词圈出来哦。

Eric's Travel Journal (2)

17th July 2019

Today is the third day of our journey. Yesterday we went on a city tour. The tour guide was very nice. She took us around the old town and showed us some landmarks, including the city hall, the central station, the harbour, and some beautiful old churches.

We came back to the guest-house after dinner. Mum couldn't find her purse in the room. She was very worried because if her ID card and driving licence were stolen, she would get in trouble. She called the local restaurant we had been to and luckily, a waiter found it. She hurried to return to the restaurant and got it back. Mum said there're always more good than bad in the world. What an experience!

Today we visited a zoo and an aquarium(水族馆). We saw many animals. My favourite is the elephant and Jenny's favourite is the dolphin. Jenny was quite surprised to know dolphins are whales, but I already learned about it in my science class. We had a good time there and we didn't leave until six.

Tomorrow we will spend all day driving to a national park. It's far away from the city but the view of nature is great. We will go camping at a campsite in the forest. Dad told us that we might see wild animals on the motorway! He also promised that he would tell us stories about the brave explorers who discovered the land. I hope we could arrive before the sun goes down—I don't want to miss the beautiful sunset!

Day 26

艾瑞克的旅行日记（二）

2019 年 7 月 17 日

今天是我们旅行的第三天。昨天我们游览了城市。导游非常亲切，她带着我们参观了老城，给我们介绍了很多地标建筑，包括市政厅、中央车站、港口，还有几座美丽的老教堂。

我们吃完晚饭后回到了宾馆。妈妈发现自己的钱包不在房间里。她非常焦急，因为如果她的身份证件和驾照被偷了，她就会遇上麻烦。她给我们去过的当地餐厅打了电话。幸运的是，一位服务员找到了钱包。她急忙返回餐厅，取回了钱包。妈妈说世界上还是好人比坏人多。这真是一段难忘的经历！

今天我们去了动物园和水族馆。我们看到了很多动物。我最喜欢的是大象，珍妮最喜欢的是海豚。她得知海豚也是一种鲸时非常惊讶，但是我已经在科学课上学过了。我们玩得很开心，直到晚上六点才离开。

明天我们将花一整天驾车去一个国家公园。它离城市非常远，但是自然风景非常棒。我们将会在森林里的一处营地露营。爸爸说我们有可能在高速公路上看到野生动物！他还答应给我们讲述发现这片土地的勇敢探险家们的故事。我希望我们可以在太阳落山之前到达——我可不想错过美丽的落日！

Word list

yesterday [ˈjestədeɪ] *n. & adv.* 昨天

tour [tʊə(r)] *n.* 旅游，旅行

tour guide 导游

station [ˈsteɪʃn] *n.* 车站；站
搭配 railway station 火车站

harbour [ˈhɑːbə(r)] *n.* 海港，港口
例句 The town has a small natural harbour. 这座城镇有一个小型的天然港口。

come [kʌm] *v.* 来；来到
搭配 come back 回来；返回

ID card 身份证
全称 identity card/identification card 身份证

drive [draɪv] *v.* 驾驶；开车 *n.* 驱车旅行；驾车路程
例句 Let's go for a drive. 咱们开车去兜风吧。

licence [ˈlaɪsns] *n.* 许可证；执照
搭配 a driving licence 驾驶执照

steal [stiːl] *v.* 偷；窃取（过去式 stole；过去分词 stolen）
例句 My wallet was stolen. 我的钱包被偷了。

trouble [ˈtrʌbl] *n.* 麻烦；困难；故障
搭配 get in trouble 陷入困境；惹上麻烦

local [ˈləʊkl] *adj.* 当地的；本地的

hurry [ˈhʌri] *v.* 仓促；匆忙，急忙
例句 The kids hurried to open their presents. 孩子们急忙打开了礼物。

return [rɪˈtɜːn] *n. & v.* 返回；退还

例句 I waited a long time for him to return. 我等他回来等了很长时间。

experience [ɪkˈspɪəriəns] *n.* 经验；经历；体验
例句 We all learn by experience. 我们都从经验中学习。

visit [ˈvɪzɪt] *v. & n.* 访问，参观
搭配 pay a visit 进行访问

zoo [zuː] *n.* 动物园

animal [ˈænɪml] *n.* 动物

elephant [ˈelɪfənt] *n.* 象
搭配 a baby elephant 幼象

dolphin [ˈdɒlfɪn] *n.* 海豚

whale [weɪl] *n.* 鲸
搭配 a blue whale 蓝鲸

already [ɔːlˈredi] *adv.* 已经，早已
例句 I'm already late. 我已经迟到了。

leave [liːv] *v.* 离开；留下（过去式/过去分词 left）
例句 I left my bags in the car. 我把包留在车里了。

until [ənˈtɪl] *prep.* 直到……为止

例句 Until 2004, she lived in Canada. 直到2004年，她一直住在加拿大。

far [fɑː(r)] *adj.* 远的；久远的

away [əˈweɪ] *adv.* 离开
搭配 be far away from 离……很远

camp [kæmp] *v.* 露营；扎营
例句 They go camping every year. 他们每年去野营。

campsite [ˈkæmpsaɪt] *n.* 野营地
助记 camp（露营）+site（地点）

wild [waɪld] *adj.* 野生的
搭配 wild animals 野生动物

motorway [ˈməʊtəweɪ] *n.* 高速公路
注意 motorway 一般用于英式英语中，美式英语中一般使用 highway。
助记 motor（汽车）+way（道路）

brave [breɪv] *adj.* 勇敢的，无畏的
例句 Be brave! 勇敢一些！

explorer [ɪkˈsplɔːrə(r)] *n.* 探险者

miss [mɪs] *v.* 错过；思念
例句 If I don't leave now I'll miss my plane. 现在不走，我就赶不上飞机了。

Exercise

1. Listen and read the phrases and sentence aloud.

   1. go on a city tour
   2. visit a zoo
   3. get in trouble
   4. brave explorers
   5. drive on the motorway
   6. dolphin and whale
   7. far away from
   8. What an experience!
   9. go camping at a campsite in the forest
   10. miss the beautiful sunset

Day 26

II. Label the pictures.

1. z _ _   2. e _ _ _ _ _ _ _   3. d _ _ _ _ _ _

4. w _ _ _ _   5. c _ _ _ _ _ _ _   6. I _ c _ _ _

7. s _ _ _ _ _ _   8. h _ _ _ _ _ _   9. m _ _ _ _ _ _ _   10. d _ _ _ _

III. For each question, write the correct answer in the gap. Write one word or a number.

Travel Plan

Father's name: Smith
Arrive in the city by: 1. _____
Where to visit on the third day: 2. _____
Where to stay on the fourth day: 3. _____

IV. **You're going to the zoo with your family next weekend. Write an email to your English friend, James.**

In your email:
- ask James to come to the zoo with your family
- say why you're going to the zoo
- tell James how you will get there

Write **25 words** or more.

_____

_____

_____

_____

_____

Unit 14
Communication

Pre-test

快速浏览下面的单词，自测一下，看看你是否已经掌握了呢？记得标记你不熟悉的单词，多多复习哦！

- ☐ clown [klaʊn] n. 小丑
- ☐ beard [bɪəd] n. （人的）胡须
- ☐ envelope ['envələʊp] n. 信封
- ☐ password ['pɑːswɜːd] n. 密码
- ☐ file [faɪl] n. 文件夹；文件
- ☐ describe [dɪ'skraɪb] v. 描述；形容
- ☐ print [prɪnt] v. 打印
- ☐ sentence ['sentəns] n. 句子
- ☐ title ['taɪtl] n. 标题，题目
- ☐ say [seɪ] v. 说；讲
- ☐ folder ['fəʊldə(r)] n. 文件夹；纸夹
- ☐ document ['dɒkjumənt] n. 文件；公文
- ☐ meeting ['miːtɪŋ] n. 会议
- ☐ loud [laʊd] adj. 响亮的；大声的
- ☐ till [tɪl] prep. 直到……为止
- ☐ pardon ['pɑːdn] exclam. 对不起；什么
- ☐ bye [baɪ] exclam. 再见；再会
- ☐ goodbye [ˌɡʊd'baɪ] exclam. 再见；再会

故事导读：
1. 小朋友，来跟 Miller 教授一起学一些与人沟通的技巧吧。
2. 记得标记一下不熟悉的单词哦。

How to Communicate Better?

Welcome to my blog! I'm Professor Miller, an expert that studies communication skills. The communication skill is probably one of the most important skills a person should have. Here is some advice to help you guys better communicate with other people.

1. Show respect. People will be more open to have long talks with you if you respect them and their ideas.

2. Listen actively. Every speaker always needs a listener. Really listen to what the other person is speaking. For example, when you're chatting with someone on the telephone, don't text at the same time.

3. Ask questions and repeat. Asking questions means you have followed what the other person said, while repeating back before sharing your opinions shows that you really understand them.

4. Make eye contact. Looking at the other person in the eye is very important when having a meaningful conversation. It helps you keep focused.

5. Cut conversation fillers. Don't use "ah" or "um" to fill the silence when you're telling a story. You will sound more confident, especially when you're trying to persuade someone.

6. Be brief, but specific. You'd better practise being short but clear in all forms of communication. Details are important, but don't bother other people by giving too much information. As a teen, it is especially helpful when you're asking

something from an adult.

7. Put away devices. Remember when you meet someone, it's quite impolite to answer calls or check text messages while he or she is talking to you.

怎样更好地沟通？

参考译文

欢迎来到我的博客！我是米勒教授，是研究沟通技巧的专家。沟通技巧可能是一个人应该掌握的最重要的技巧之一。这里有一些可以帮助你们更好地与别人沟通的建议。

1. 表示尊重。如果你尊重对方和对方的想法，他们会更愿意和你促膝长谈。

2. 积极聆听。每个讲话的人都需要一个倾听者。要真正地倾听对方在说什么。比如说，如果你正在打电话聊天，就不要同时给其他人发短信。

3. 提问并重复。提问意味着你认真听了对方所说的话，而在分享你自己的观点之前重复一遍别人说过的话则显示你真正理解了对方。

4. 进行眼神交流。开展一段有意义的谈话时，看着对方的眼睛是极其重要的，这会帮助你集中注意力。

5. 去掉语气词。当你讲故事时，不要用"啊"或"嗯"来填补沉默。这样你会听上去更自信，特别是当你试图说服别人的时候。

6. 要简练，但要说到点子上。在各种形式的沟通中，你最好练习做到简短且清晰。细节很重要，但是不要给出过多的信息以至于让别人感到困扰。十几岁的青少年在向一个成年人要东西的时候，这一点特别有用。

7. 拿开电子设备。记住，当你与某人见面时，如果他/她正在和你说话，此时你接电话或查看短信是非常无礼的。

Word list

blog [blɒg] *n.* 博客；网络日志
搭配 a video blog 视频博客

probably ['prɒbəbli] *adv.* 大概；或许；很可能
例句 You're probably right. 你很可能是对的。

person ['pɜːsn] *n.* 人
例句 He's just the person we need for the job. 他正是我们需要的适合这项工作的人。

here [hɪə(r)] *adv.* 在这里
例句 Come over here. 过来吧。

advice [əd'vaɪs] *n.* 建议；忠告
注意 advice 为不可数名词。
例句 Let me give you a piece of advice. 让我给你一个忠告。

help [help] *v. & n.* 帮助
例句 He always helps with the housework. 他总是帮着做家务。

communicate [kəˈmjuːnɪkeɪt] v. 交流；沟通
搭配 communicate with each other 相互沟通

long [lɒŋ] adj. 长时间的；长的；远的
搭配 a long film 放映时间长的电影
　　 a long walk 长途步行

speaker [ˈspiːkə(r)] n. 演讲者；说话者
搭配 a native speaker of English 以英语为母语的人

speak [spiːk] v. 说话；演讲
例句 Do you speak English? 你会说英语吗？

example [ɪɡˈzɑːmpl] n. 例子；榜样
搭配 for example 例如

chat [tʃæt] v. & n. 聊天，闲谈
例句 I had a long chat with her. 我和她闲聊了很久。

telephone [ˈtelɪfəʊn] n. 电话
例句 The telephone rang and Pat answered it. 电话铃响了，帕特接了电话。

text [tekst] v. 发短信 n. 文本；课文
例句 Text me when you're on your way. 你在路上给我发短信吧。

ask [ɑːsk] v. 询问；要求
例句 He asked about her family. 他询问了她的家庭情况。

question [ˈkwestʃən] n. 问题；疑问
搭配 ask/answer a question 提出/回答问题

repeat [rɪˈpiːt] v. 重复
例句 I'm sorry—could you repeat that? 对不起——你可以再说一遍吗？

follow [ˈfɒləʊ] v. 跟随；遵循
例句 Why didn't you follow my advice? 你为什么不听我的劝告？

while [waɪl] conj. 与……同时；然而
例句 You can go swimming while I'm having lunch. 我吃午饭时你可以去游泳。

share [ʃeə(r)] v. 分享
例句 Eli shared his chocolate with the other kids. 伊莱把他的巧克力和其他孩子一起分着吃了。

opinion [əˈpɪnjən] n. 意见；看法
搭配 in my opinion 依我看来；在我看来

understand [ˌʌndəˈstænd] v. 理解；懂
例句 I don't understand what he's saying. 我不明白他在说些什么。

contact [ˈkɒntækt] v. & n. 联系；联络
例句 I've been trying to contact you all day. 我一整天都在设法与你联系。

conversation [ˌkɒnvəˈseɪʃn] n. 交谈，会话
例句 This is a private conversation. 这是一段私人谈话。

fill [fɪl] v. 装满；使充满
例句 Smoke filled the room. 房间里烟雾弥漫。

tell [tel] v. 告诉；讲述
搭配 tell a story 讲故事

story [ˈstɔːri] n. 故事
搭配 a bedtime story 睡前故事

sound [saʊnd] v. 听起来好像
例句 His voice sounded strange on the phone. 他的声音在电话里听着挺怪的。

persuade [pəˈsweɪd] v. 说服，劝说
例句 Please try and persuade her. 请尽力说服她。

short [ʃɔːt] adj. 简短的；短的
搭配 a short skirt 短裙

clear [klɪə(r)] adj. 清楚的；清澈的
例句 Are these instructions clear enough? 这些说明足够清楚吗？

form [fɔːm] *n.* 形式；种类
搭配 different life forms 不同的生命形式

detail ['diːteɪl] *n.* 细节，琐事
例句 I can't go into details now. 我现在不能细说。

bother ['bɒðə(r)] *v.* 烦扰，打扰
例句 Sorry to bother you. 很抱歉打扰你。

give [gɪv] *v.* 给；提供
例句 Give your mother the letter. 把信给你母亲。

information [ˌɪnfə'meɪʃn] *n.* 信息
搭配 a piece of information 一则消息

adult ['ædʌlt] *n.* 成年人
例句 Children must be accompanied by an adult. 儿童必须有成年人陪同。

meet [miːt] *v.* 遇见；会见（过去式/过去分词 met）
例句 Maybe we'll meet again sometime. 说不定我们什么时候还会再次见面。

quite [kwaɪt] *adv.* 很；相当
例句 He plays quite well. 他表现得相当好。

call [kɔːl] *v. & n.* 打电话
搭配 give somebody a call 给某人打电话

message ['mesɪdʒ] *n.* 消息
例句 He sent me a text message. 他给我发了一条短信。

talk [tɔːk] *v. & n.* 说话；讲话
例句 The baby is just starting to talk. 这个婴儿刚开始咿呀学语。

Exercise

Ⅰ. Listen and read the phrases aloud.

1. ask a question
2. tell a story
3. have a conversation
4. share an opinion
5. follow and repeat
6. meet an adult
7. a piece of information
8. call and text
9. short and clear
10. give a person some advice

Ⅱ. Label the pictures.

1. t _ _ _
2. t _ _ _
3. c _ _ _

4. t _ _ _ _ _ _ _ _   5. s _ _ _ _ _ _   6. r _ _ _ _ _

7. f _ _ _ _ _   8. s _ _ _ _

9. s _ _ _ _   10. c _ _ _ _

Ⅲ. Listen and choose the correct answer for each question.

1. Why does Eric give Marie a call?
   A. To chat with her.
   B. To ask for information about an exam.
   C. To tell her the teacher's information.
2. When can Eric sign up for this year's exam?
   A. In January.   B. In May.   C. Not given.
3. If Eric wants to sign up for the exam, what should he do?
   A. Make a phone call.   B. Send a text message.   C. Fill up a form online.

IV. Answer the questions.

1. When do you usually chat with your friends?

   _____

   _____

2. How do you usually chat with your friends?

   _____

   _____

3. What should you do when you are communicating with the other person?

   _____

   _____

故事导读：
1. 小朋友，你知道怎样结交新朋友又不失去老朋友吗？来看看 Miller 教授给你的建议吧。
2. 如果有不认识的单词，记得要用笔圈出来哦。

Professor Miller's Advice on Friendship

Friendship is very important, but it's also among the most difficult relationships to make and keep in our life.

How to be a good friend?

- Be respectful. If your friends said something you don't agree with, don't argue with them or shout at them. If you show your respect, they will tell you the reasons why they feel that way and discuss a new point with you.
- Be kind. If your friends happened to do something wrong, choose your words carefully to explain and do not let them have a deep sense of shame. If they apologised, excuse their mistakes.
- Give each other some space. Your best friends cannot always be in company with you. Sometimes they also need other friends. So learn to go out alone or make a date with other friends.

How to make new friends?

- Smile more; laugh more. Smiles and laughters tell people that you're friendly and easy-going.
- Be open-minded. It's easier to make friends with similar interests in the class or the same department. However, isn't it more interesting to have friends from online chatrooms or different departments?

How to keep old friends?

- Keep in touch. It's easy to know your friends' latest news through modern technologies. A quick note with a few words, a greeting with emoji or sharing a funny picture on social media show that you still care about them, and you want to continue your relationship. It's also nice to write a congratulation postcard or prepare a present like puzzles for them on special days as a symbol of your long-lasting friendship!

- Go with the flow. You might feel lost when you cannot see your friends very often. However, distance doesn't make real differences to them. They're still the same as before, and your friendship won't end.

米勒教授关于友谊的建议

友谊很重要，但它也是我们生活中最难建立和保持的关系之一。

怎样做一个好朋友？

- 要尊重朋友。如果你的朋友说了一些你并不认同的话，不要与他们争论或是吵嚷。如果你表现出尊重的态度，他们会讲清楚自己那么想的原因，并且和你讨论看待事物的新角度。
- 要善良。如果你的朋友碰巧做了一些错事，要谨慎用词进行说明，不要让他们有深深的愧疚感。如果他们道歉了，那就原谅他们的错误吧。
- 给彼此一些空间。你的好朋友不可能总是陪伴在你身边。有时他们也需要其他朋友。所以你要学会独自外出或与其他朋友相约。

怎样结识新朋友？

- 多微笑，多大笑。微笑和笑声告诉别人你是友善的、好相处的。
- 敞开心扉。在同一个班级或同一个部门结交兴趣相投的朋友更容易。然而，从线上聊天室或不同部门结识朋友不是更有趣吗？

如何维护老朋友？

- 保持联系。通过现代科技很容易了解朋友的最新消息。几个字的简单留言，带着表情符号的问候，或者是在社交媒体上分享一张有趣的图片，这些都意味着你依旧在乎对方，想让你们的友情继续下去。在特殊的日子里给他们写一张祝贺明信片或准备一份智力游戏之类的礼物，作为你们长久友谊的象征，也是不错的。
- 顺其自然。你不能时常与朋友见面可能会感觉很失落。然而距离并不会真正改变他们。他们依然一如既往，而你们的友谊也不会结束。

Word list

among [ə'mʌn] *prep.* 在（三者或以上）中
例句 Bees buzzed lazily among the flowers. 蜜蜂在花丛中懒洋洋地嗡嗡鸣叫着。

agree [ə'griː] *v.* 同意，赞成
搭配 agree with sb 同意某人的意见
例句 I couldn't agree more. 我完全同意。

argue ['ɑːgjuː] *v.* 争论，争辩
例句 My brothers are always arguing. 我的兄弟们总是争论不休。

shout [ʃaʊt] *v.* 喊叫；大声说
搭配 shout at sb 对某人大声喊叫
例句 Stop shouting and listen! 别嚷了，听着！

reason ['riːzn] *n.* 理由；原因
搭配 for some reason 出于某种原因

discuss [dɪ'skʌs] *v.* 讨论
搭配 discuss sth with sb 和某人讨论某事

happen ['hæpən] *v.* （偶然）发生；碰巧
搭配 happen to 碰巧
例句 Accidents like this happen all the time. 此类事故一直在发生。

choose [tʃuːz] *v.* 选择（过去式 chose；过去分词 chosen）
例句 We chose to go by train. 我们选择乘火车去。

explain [ɪk'spleɪn] *v.* 说明；解释
搭配 explain the reason why... 解释……的原因

shame [ʃeɪm] *n.* 羞耻，羞愧
例句 She felt a deep sense of shame. 她深感羞耻。

excuse [ɪk'skjuːs] *v.* 原谅；宽恕
搭配 excuse me 劳驾，请原谅

例句 Please excuse the mess. 这里凌乱不堪，请见谅。

company ['kʌmpəni] *n.* 公司；陪伴
例句 I enjoy Joe's company. 我喜欢和乔在一起。

alone [ə'ləʊn] *adj.* 独自的 *adv.* 独自地
例句 It was her first experience of living alone. 那是她第一次独自生活。

laugh [lɑːf] *v.* 笑
搭配 laugh at 嘲笑

department [dɪ'pɑːtmənt] *n.* （大学的）系；部门
搭配 a government department 政府部门

chatroom ['tʃætruːm] *n.* 聊天室
助记 chat（聊天）+ room（房间）

news [njuːz] *n.* 新闻；消息
例句 What's the latest news? 有什么最新消息吗？

modern ['mɒdn] *adj.* 现代的
搭配 modern technology 现代科技

quick [kwɪk] *adj.* 快的；迅速的
例句 It's quicker by train. 坐火车更快。

word [wɜːd] *n.* 单词
例句 Do not write more than 100 words. 写的东西不要超过100词。

emoji [ɪ'məʊdʒi] *n.* 表情符号

funny ['fʌni] *adj.* 有趣的；滑稽的
搭配 a funny story 滑稽的故事

media ['miːdiə] *n.* 媒体
搭配 social media 社交媒体

still [stɪl] *adv.* 仍然；还
例句 Mum, I'm still hungry! 妈妈，我还饿！

continue [kənˈtɪnjuː] v. 继续，延续
例句 The rain continued all afternoon. 这场雨连续下了整整一下午。

also [ˈɔːlsəʊ] adv. 也；而且

congratulation [kənˌɡrætʃuˈleɪʃn] n. 祝贺；贺词
例句 Congratulations on your exam results! 祝贺你考出了好成绩！

postcard [ˈpəʊstkɑːd] n. 明信片
助记 post（邮寄）+card（卡片）
例句 Send us a postcard from Venice! 从威尼斯给我们寄张明信片！

prepare [prɪˈpeə(r)] v. 准备
搭配 prepare for 为……准备

present [ˈpreznt] n. 礼物 adj. 当前的
搭配 birthday presents 生日礼物

puzzle [ˈpʌzl] n. 谜；智力游戏
搭配 a crossword puzzle 纵横字谜

symbol [ˈsɪmbl] n. 象征；符号
例句 The dove is a universal symbol of peace. 鸽子是和平的普遍象征。

lost [lɒst] adj. 迷路的；丢失的；迷惘的
例句 We would be lost without your help. 没有你的帮助，我们会迷路的。

real [ˈriːəl] adj. 实际的；真实的

difference [ˈdɪfrəns] n. 差异；不同
例句 I can never tell the differences between the twins. 我从来都分不清这对双胞胎。

end [end] v. & n. 结束
搭配 come to an end 结束
at the end of the week 在周末

Exercise

I. Listen and read the phrases aloud.

1. laugh at a funny story
2. prepare for a meeting
3. agree with someone's opinion
4. shout at someone
5. argue with someone
6. explain the reasons
7. tell the differences
8. come to an end
9. a sense of shame
10. alone and lost

II. Match the words with the Chinese meanings.

Group 1

1. agree   A. 解释
2. argue   B. 同意
3. shout   C. 争论
4. discuss   D. 喊叫
5. explain   E. 讨论

Group 2

1. shame   A. 选择
2. choose   B. 羞愧
3. present   C. 发笑
4. laugh   D. 滑稽的
5. funny   E. 礼物

III. Listen and choose the correct answer for each question.

1. What did the boy once send his sister?

   A　　　　　　　　　　　　　B

2. What does the boy want to send his friend?

   A　　　　　　　　　　　　　B

3. Which one is the symbol of peace?

   A　　　　　　　　　　　　　B

IV. Your friend Ryan has moved to another city and you want to contact him. Write an email to Ryan.

In your email:
- tell Ryan how everything is going on in your life
- ask him whether he has made any new friends
- tell him how you will keep in touch with him

Write **25 words** or more.

_____

_____

_____

_____

参考答案

Unit 1

Day 1

Ⅰ．（略）

Ⅱ．
1. grandfather/grandpa 2. grandmother/grandma 3. mother/mum/mummy
4. father/dad/daddy 5. aunt 6. uncle 7. sister 8. brother 9. cousins

Ⅲ．
1. A 2. B 3. A

Ⅳ．（答案仅供参考）
1. There're four people in my family.
2. My mum, my dad, my sister and I.
3. Yes. I love everyone in my family.

听力原文

Ⅲ．
1. Girl: Hi John! How many members are there in your family?
   Boy: There are six: my parents, my grandparents, my sister and I.
2. Woman: I can't find Amy and John. Do you know what they are doing now?
   Man: Amy is doing the homework and John is writing a letter to his pen-friend.
3. Man: Lucy, your grandpa will come to visit us this Friday.
   Girl: Great! How about Grandma?
   Man: She has to see the doctor on Friday, so she will not come.

Day 2

Ⅰ．（略）

Ⅱ．
1. kid 2. friendly 3. kiss 4. gift 5. balloon
6. neighbour 7. birthday 8. lovely 9. teenager 10. memory

Ⅲ．
1. 8 2. balloons 3. book

Ⅳ．（答案仅供参考）

Hi，Andy，

My name is Dan and I'm 11 years old. I live in Beijing. There're five people in my family: my parents，my grandparents and me. I have many good friends.

Best wishes，

Dan

听力原文

Ⅲ．

I am Mrs Haywood and next Saturday is my daughter Emma's 13th birthday. I am going to prepare a birthday party for her at our house. I will invite Emma's grandpa and grandma，uncle and aunt，as well as her friends John，Harriet，Peter and Nick. I will bake a lovely chocolate cake and pick up some flowers from the backyard. Emma's dad will buy candles and balloons from the shop. The gift we prepared for her is a book about sailing. We hope she will like the gift and enjoy the party.

Unit 2

Day 3

Ⅰ．（略）

Ⅱ．

1. garden 2. garage 3. gate 4. rubbish bin 5. living room

6. sofa 7. carpet 8. bookcase 9. television

10. chair 11. oven 12. fridge 13. cupboard 14. drawer

Ⅲ．

1. C 2. A 3. B

Ⅳ．（答案仅供参考）

1. There are 6 rooms in my house: a large living room，three bedrooms，a dinning room and a kitchen.

2. I watch TV in the living room.

3. We have dinner in the dining room.

听力原文

Ⅲ．

1. Boy: Mum, I can't find my English textbook. Did you see it?

   Woman: Yes, I did. You left it on the sofa and I just put it in your bag.

2. Girl: Grandpa, how many guests do we have today? Do I need to get more plates from the drawer?

   Man: We have a dinner for 8 people. Could you please take 2 more plates?

   Girl: Certainly.

3. Woman: Hey Jack. Where do you and your family usually have dinner at home?

   Man: We usually have dinner in the kitchen. But yesterday my uncle and aunt visited us, so we had dinner in the dining room.

Day 4

Ⅰ.（略）

Ⅱ.
1. bedroom 2. bed 3. pillow 4. sheet 5. blanket
6. lamp 7. stair 8. clock 9. armchair 10. bathroom
11. toilet 12. shower 13. bathtub 14. shampoo 15. towel

Ⅲ.
1. B 2. A 3. A

Ⅳ.（答案仅供参考）

I live in a big house. It has a living room, a dining room, a kitchen and three bedrooms. At six o'clock, my mum is cooking dinner for us in the kitchen. Dad is watching television in the living room. My brother is playing football in the yard and I am doing my homework in my bedroom. After half an hour, the dinner is ready and we have dinner together in the dining room.

听力原文

Ⅲ.
1. Woman: Hey Ivan, do you have to share a room with your brother?
   Boy: Not anymore. He doesn't live at home now. But there're still two beds in my room.
2. Woman: Mr Smith, I heard that your family have fixed reading time every week. It sounds really great! I also want to do that with my family. Do you read books together in the living room?
   Man: Oh, it would be wonderful. Actually, we read books together in my bedroom. It's more relaxing and cosier.
3. Boy: Mum, can I use the bathtub today?
   Woman: Darling, I'm afraid you can't. It needs repairing. You have to use the shower.

Unit 3

Day 5

Ⅰ.（略）

Ⅱ.
1. school 2. classroom 3. blackboard 4. student 5. get up
6. mistake 7. guidebook 8. mark 9. read 10. write

Ⅲ.
1. B 2. A 3. C

Ⅳ.（答案仅供参考）

1. Yes, I do. I like going to school every day.
2. There are 25 students in my class.
3. My favourite subjects are English and science.

听力原文

Ⅲ.

Samantha: Good afternoon, Karl! How are you doing?

Karl: To be honest, not good. I failed the maths exam.

Samantha: I'm sorry to hear that. I have to say I'm quite good at maths and I got a good mark this time. I can help you with your maths after class if you want.

Karl: That would be great! Thank you so much, Samantha.

Samantha: Never mind. I know history is your favourite subject. Can you help me with the history homework?

Karl: Certainly. Oh, it's time for PE class. Mr Johnson left school last week. Have you met our new teacher yet?

Samantha: Yes. He is Mr Blair.

 Day 6

Ⅰ. (略)

Ⅱ.

Group 1

1. C   2. D   3. B   4. E   5. A

Group 2

1. E   2. C   3. A   4. B   5. D

Ⅲ.

1. B   2. C   3. C

Ⅳ. (答案仅供参考)

Hello Ethan!

I'm also a fifth-grade student. I study in XXX Primary School. My favourite subjects are biology and maths. I am very good at them. I bring my textbooks, notebooks, pencils, rubber and ruler to school every day.

Best wishes,

(Your name)

听力原文

Ⅲ.

1. Christina: Ann. Can I borrow your maths textbook for a while?

   Ann: Sorry Christina. I have lent it to Mike.

2. Woman: Bobby, the floor and the desks are so dirty. Do you know who's on duty to clean them today?

   Boy: Today Danny should clean the floor and Jane should clean the desks.

3. Woman: Ben, you are late for class again. You should arrive before 8:20 a.m. You're 15 minutes late.

   Boy: I'm sorry, Mrs Thompson. I will never be late.

Unit 4

✓ Day 7

Ⅰ．（略）

Ⅱ．

1. T-shirt   2. blouse   3. shorts   4. trousers   5. boots

6. jacket   7. skirt   8. jumper   9. coat   10. model

Ⅲ．

1. A   2. B   3. A

Ⅳ．（答案仅供参考）

1. Yes, I do. I like shopping for clothes. ／No, I don't. I don't like shopping for clothes.

2. I usually go shopping with my parents.

3. I'm wearing a T-shirt and a pair of trousers.

听力原文

Ⅲ．

1. Martin：Good morning, Jack! I like your T-shirt. It looks great!

   Jack：Thank you, Martin. I went shopping with my mum and sister yesterday and my mum bought me this new T-shirt.

2. Daisy：Mum, have you seen my skirt? I want to wear it to school.

   Mum：Sorry, Daisy, I have washed it. I'm afraid you have to wear trousers.

3. Girl：Do you know Jacob? I found a notebook. His name is on it. I think he lost it.

   Boy：Jacob is over there. He wears a striped T-shirt.

✓ Day 8

Ⅰ．（略）

Ⅱ．

Group 1

1. D   2. C   3. B   4. E   5. A

Group 2

1. D   2. C   3. E   4. A   5. B

1. 9:30   2. first   3. cheque

Ⅳ．（答案仅供参考）

A girl in a skirt went shopping with her mother. They walked into a clothes shop. There are many beautiful clothes in the latest fashion in the shop. She chose a T-shirt and a pair of trousers and tried them on. She looked very pretty in the mirror. Her mother paid by credit card for the new clothes and the girl was very happy.

听力原文

Ⅲ.

Welcome to the Capital Mall. Today is Sunday, on the 24th of September. Our opening time will be from 10 a.m. to 9:30 p.m. On the ground floor, we offer our customers jewellery and accessories. You can also buy make-up products on this floor. On the first floor, we have clothing stores for everyone in your family—for men, women and children. We hope all customers can enjoy their shopping. However, we're very sorry to inform you that we don't accept cheques now. Please pay by credit card or in cash. Thank you very much for your understanding.

Unit 5

✓ Day 9

Ⅰ.（略）

Ⅱ.
1. cake   2. apple   3. banana   4. mango   5. strawberry   6. lemon
7. table   8. bowl   9. plate   10. spoon   11. fork   12. cup

Ⅲ.
1. A   2. C   3. A

Ⅳ.（答案仅供参考）

1. I usually eat apples, bananas, mangoes and strawberries.
2. I usually have rice, fresh vegetables and meat, and delicious desserts for dinner.
3. I usually use a knife, fork and spoon to have dinner. Sometimes I use chopsticks.

听力原文

Ⅲ.

1. Girl: Hey Jack, my mum put a banana and an orange in my meal box but I am too full to eat them now. Do you want to have one?

   Jack: Thank you so much. But I only like apples.

2. Girl: Hi Josh, Tom will have a birthday party tomorrow. I will bake a strawberry cake and Cecelia will bring some home-made chocolate biscuits.

   Josh: I'm going to make some cream cupcakes tonight. Can't wait to share them with you guys!

3. Man: Excuse me? I don't want to drink coffee or tea. Is there anything else?

   Waitress: Yes. Would you like to have a glass of orange juice?

✓ Day 10

Ⅰ.（略）

Ⅱ.

Group 1

1. D   2. C   3. B   4. E   5. A

Group 2

1. B   2. D   3. E   4. C   5. A

Ⅲ.

1. C   2. A   3. D

Ⅳ.（答案仅供参考）

Hi Juno,

My name is Tao and I live in China. My favourite food is chicken burger. On weekends, we usually have noodles or dumplings for dinner. Both of my parents cook. They like making food.

Best wishes,

Tao

听力原文

Ⅲ.

Charles: Hey Susan! Andrew and I are going to a fast food shop to get some food for supper. Is there anything you want to eat?

Susan: That is great! I'm hungry now. I would like to have some mushroom soup with bread.

Charles: Mushroom soup…Let me see…I'm sorry it's not on the menu.

Susan: How about a sausage pizza?

Charles: OK! So I'm going to order a sausage pizza for you, a beef sandwich for Andrew, and a burger with some chips for myself.

Susan: Thanks a lot! How much does it cost?

Charles: Never mind. It's $11.

Unit 6

 Day 11

Ⅰ.（略）

Ⅱ.

Group 1

1. C   2. A   3. D   4. E   5. B

Group 2

1. B   2. C   3. E   4. A   5. D

Ⅲ.

1. C   2. B   3. A

Ⅳ.（答案仅供参考）

1. My favourite sport is football, because it's well-known.

2. Yes, I've been a big fan of Messi for several years./No, I haven't. I hardly watch sports matches. So I don't know any players.

3. Beijing Olympic Games was held in 2008.

听力原文

Ⅲ.

1. Girl: Last night the football match in Canada was fantastic. Did you watch it?

   Boy: Sure, French team was so good although Spanish team won the match.

2. Anna: Hey Tom, will you be free on Friday?

   Tom: Yes, I think so.

   Anna: What about going to watch a diving match with me?

   Tom: That will be great. Let's tell Mum about our plan.

3. Man: Hey, why don't you go swimming?

   Boy: Strong sunlight makes me sick, and I'm frightened by huge waves.

   Man: OK, then stay on the beach and don't go around.

Day 12

Ⅰ.（略）

Ⅱ.

1. basketball   2. volleyball   3. table tennis   4. baseball   5. tennis

6. badminton   7. skiing   8. skate   9. bicycle   10. climbing

Ⅲ.

1. A   2. B   3. A

Ⅳ.（答案仅供参考）

1. I want to try diving most, because I'm so curious about the world under the sea.

2. Yes, I joined the volleyball team when I was in high school. /No, I haven't.

3. I will put chocolate, a clean towel and several bottles of water in it.

听力原文

Ⅲ.

Woman: Hi, did you watch the baseball match last night? It was England versus Canada.

Man: You mean the one held in Singapore? Sure, I am very happy because England won the match. You know, England is my homeland.

Woman: Oh, as a Canadian, I like tennis the most. I play tennis with my friends in the sports centre every weekend. Would you like to come and play with us?

Man: That sounds great! When will we meet?

Woman: 10 o'clock, Sunday morning. Will you be free at that time?

Man: Yes, see you on Sunday!

Unit 7

Day 13

Ⅰ.（略）

Ⅱ.

    1. chess   2. stamp   3. guitar   4. music   5. violin

    6. sing   7. read   8. draw   9. piano   10. film

Ⅲ.

    1. B   2. B   3. A

Ⅳ.（答案仅供参考）

    1. My hobbies are music, photography, and drawing.

    2. My best friend is Alice. She likes collecting stamps, painting and photography.

    3. Yes, I do. My father likes singing and my mother likes playing the violin. ／No, I don't. I will go back home to ask my parents.

听力原文

Ⅲ.

    Amy: Hi! Tommy, what are you going to do?

    Tommy: I am going to have guitar lessons.

    Amy: How often do you have them?

    Tommy: Twice a week. Playing the guitar is my favourite hobby. Can you play any instruments, Amy?

    Amy: Yes. I can play the violin. My father often teaches me to play it at home. I practice a lot.

    Tommy: That's great! Your father must like music.

    Amy: Yes, he can also sing some wonderful songs. I enjoy listening to his singing.

    Tommy: I hope I can listen to his singing someday.

Day 14

Ⅰ.（略）

Ⅱ.

    1. police officer   2. doctor   3. painter   4. teacher   5. businessman   6. writer

    7. dancer   8. pilot   9. mechanic   10. engineer   11. actor   12. journalist

Ⅲ.

    1. D   2. B   3. A

Ⅳ.（答案仅供参考）

Hi, Jack!

My hobbies are reading and listening to music. I like reading magazines, newspapers and comics. I also enjoy listening to pop music, hip hop, jazz and rap. In the future I would like to be a teacher, because I want to share my knowledge with more people.

Best wishes,

（Your name）

听力原文

Ⅲ.

Rose：What is your occupation now, Tony?

Tony：I am a primary school teacher now. What about you, Rose?

Rose：I was a writer two years ago. Now I am a journalist.

Tony：That is a big change for your life. I am so happy for you. Do you know what Amy is doing now? I haven't seen her for a long time. I heard that she went to New York and dreamed to be an actress.

Rose：Oh, Amy gave up her dream of being an actress. She is a dentist now.

Tony：That is great. She is really a gentle girl and always willing to help others.

Unit 8

✓ Day 15

Ⅰ.（略）

Ⅱ.

1. north   2. west   3. south   4. east   5. left

6. right   7. front   8. behind   9. upstairs   10. downstairs

Ⅲ.

1. A   2. B   3. A

（答案仅供参考）

1. Yes, I can. There are four main directions: north, south, east and west.

2. The sun rises in the east and sets in the west.

3. My home faces south.

听力原文

Ⅲ.

1. Man：Good morning, Luna! Have you seen Jamie? I can't find him anywhere.

   Girl：I just saw him sitting in the front of the classroom reading a book. I think he's still there.

2. Man：Excuse me? I'm looking for the library. I was told that it is at the corner of Belleview Road and Market Street, but I can't find it.

   Woman：The library? No, it's at the end of Belleview Road. Just go straight along this road for about five minutes and you'll see it on your right.

3. Woman：It's so cold outside! Where're the kids?

   Man：They are playing upstairs. They built a snowman just now. It is too cold to play outside. I asked them to come back.

Day 16

Ⅰ．（略）

Ⅱ．

Group 1

1．C　　2．E　　3．A　　4．D　　5．B

Group 2

1．B　　2．E　　3．D　　4．A　　5．C

Ⅲ．

1．B　　2．A　　3．A

Ⅳ．（答案仅供参考）

A tourist who carried a heavy backpack got lost in London. He was holding a map but couldn't find his way to the museum. Luckily, an old lady who passed by helped him. She told him that he should go straight along the main road, and then turn right at the second traffic light, and the museum is on his left.

听力原文

Ⅲ．

1. Boy：Excuse me, madam? I'm going to the city centre. Should I get on Bus 11?

   Woman：No. It's the wrong direction. You should go to the opposite bus station and wait for Bus 12.

2. Man：Hi, honey. Where're you? I am waiting for you at the east gate.

   Woman：What? Are you kidding me? I am at the north gate waiting for you.

   Man：Wait for a few minutes. I'll go to find you.

3. Girl：Mum, shall we go to the grocery store this afternoon? There is little milk in the fridge.

   Woman：This afternoon I have to go to the hospital to see a doctor. I will write a shopping list and your dad will take you to the grocery store.

Unit 9

Day 17

Ⅰ．（略）

Ⅱ．

Group 1

1．D　　2．E　　3．B　　4．A　　5．C

Group 2

1．B　　2．D　　3．E　　4．A　　5．C

1．A　　2．A　　3．C

Ⅳ．（答案仅供参考）

1. Yes, I am. I have many electronic products at my home, such as computers, smartphones, MP3 players, and digital cameras. ／ No, I am not. I think electronic products are bad for my eyes.

2. No. I have never written a letter to my best friend. But we often use apps like Wechat, QQ and Twitter to communicate.
3. We haven't seen each other for a long time. I miss you so much. I have lots of interesting things to tell you.

听力原文

Ⅲ.
1. Joy: Where is Judy? I can't find her everywhere.
   Belly: Oh, she went to a book exhibition in the morning. Now she is mailing her parents letters in the post office.
2. Dan: I went to a shopping mall yesterday with my father and he bought me a new smartphone as a birthday gift.
   Mary: That's great. I received a book as a birthday present from my parents last year.
3. Julie: Hey, Peter. Do you know when and where the party will be held this week?
   Peter: The party will be held in my house this Saturday night. I will send you an email to tell you more details about the party.

Day 18

Ⅰ. （略）

Ⅱ.
1. computer　　2. mouse　　3. keyboard　　4. printer　　5. memory card
6. laptop　　7. video　　8. digital camera

Ⅲ.
1. A　　2. B　　3. A

Ⅳ. （答案仅供参考）

Hi, Jackson!

I am so pleased that you have your laptop. There is a computer at my home. I usually use it to listen to music and watch some funny videos or video courses. It's not hard for me to upload some videos or my homework to the computer.

Best wishes,

（Your name）

听力原文

Ⅲ.

Penny: Leo, have you heard a vlogger on the social media named "Science Tom"? I have watched a lot of his videos recently.

Leo: Yes! His videos are so amusing. Those scientific experiments he did are all interesting and easy to understand.

Penny: I would like to make my own videos after watching his. But there's something wrong with my mouse. I can't start my software and website on the computer.

Leo: That's too bad. You should buy a new one. What do you want to record in your videos?

Penny：I would like to share some learning methods.

Leo：Great. They will be very useful for students. If I make videos, I think I will share how to play the piano. Anyway, I can't wait to see your works! You had better start as soon as possible.

Penny：I am going to buy a new mouse this Saturday. Will you join me?

Unit 10

✓ Day 19

Ⅰ．（略）

Ⅱ．

1. spring   2. windy   3. June   4. hot   5. rainy

6. autumn   7. cool   8. red   9. winter   10. January

Ⅲ．

1. B   2. B   3. C

Ⅳ．（答案仅供参考）

1. I was born in November. My best friend Jessica was born in June.

2. My favourite season is summer. Because I love going to the beach and swimming in the sea.

3. I prefer rainy weather. Because I enjoy reading a book by the window and listening to the raindrops.

听力原文

Ⅲ．

From the blooming in spring to the first snowfall in winter, every season in London is beautiful. Here's some helpful advice for your trip. Winter in London is usually cold and rainy. Be sure to pack a winter coat with a hat, gloves, and a scarf. In spring, the weather becomes warm and sunny but still cold and rainy sometimes. In summer, it is generally pleasant, but at night it is a little cold, so don't forget to pack a light jacket. Once in a while, heavy rain and thunderstorms appear in the afternoons. Warm weather usually lasts through September before the temperatures begin to drop sharply in October. Autumn is usually London's rainiest season. No matter when you come to London, remember to be prepared for wet weather!

✓ Day 20

Ⅰ．（略）

Ⅱ．

1. moon   2. star   3. mountain   4. grass

5. lake   6. cloud   7. island   8. forest

Ⅲ．

1. B   2. C   3. C

Ⅳ．（答案仅供参考）

Hello Elena,

I'm going to the national park with my parents on Saturday. Would you like to come with us? Summer is the best season to visit the park. We're going to see beautiful mountains, lakes and clouds. The weather will be sunny, but it might rain at noon. So don't forget to bring a raincoat or an umbrella.

Looking forward to hearing from you!

Best wishes,

(Your name)

听力原文

Ⅲ.
1. Aimee: Jared, you don't seem well. Your face is pale. Do you need any help?
   Jared: Thank you, Aimee. I have had a headache for three days and I will go to see the doctor on Wednesday.
2. Mum: Jason! Don't forget to bring your umbrella to school. The weather report shows it will be rainy in the afternoon.
   Jason: Really? It's sunny now and there're even no clouds in the sky. But anyway, I will take it with me. Just in case.
3. Woman: Excuse me? I just lost my purse at the store when I was shopping with my husband. It's black and it has some silver decorations on it. Have you seen it?
   Man: I'm really sorry to hear that, Madam. But today we've only collected two lost purses; one is red and the other is blue. You can leave your name and your phone number, and we will contact you when your purse is found.

Unit 11

Day 21

Ⅰ. (略)

Ⅱ.
1. film   2. boring   3. invitation   4. idea   5. guess
6. party   7. afraid   8. different   9. scooter 10. worry

Ⅲ.
1. B   2. C   3. C

Ⅳ. (答案仅供参考)
1. Yes, I often receive invitations from my friends to take part in their birthday parties.
2. I prefer to go out with friends rather than stay at home on the weekend. If there is nothing to do, it will be boring to stay at home.
3. I will watch films or do some outdoor sports with my friends.

听力原文

Ⅲ.
1. Girl: Hey Tom, would you like to go swimming with me tomorrow?

Boy：That's great. I'll be free after 10 a.m., but I must do my homework at 6 p.m.

　　Girl：OK, see you at 11 a.m. at the school gate.

2. Man：Did you enjoy the party?

　　Woman：Yes! That was wonderful. The music was just perfect.

　　Man：Really? The music made me mad. It was awfully noisy!

3. Man：Were you invited to Nancy's wedding this Saturday?

　　Woman：Yes, I booked a hotel room near the sea, so I can walk to the wedding place.

　　Man：Wonderful. I didn't book a hotel room, so I have to ride a scooter to the wedding place.

✓ Day 22

Ⅰ.（略）

Ⅱ.

Group 1

1. C　　2. D　　3. E　　4. A　　5. B

Group 2

1. D　　2. A　　3. B　　4. E　　5. C

Ⅲ.

1. B　　2. C　　3. C

Ⅳ.（答案仅供参考）

　　The girl received a phone call from her friend. Her friend wanted to invite her to watch a film. They went to the cinema and chose a horror film to watch. The plots and background music were rather scary. However, they were not scared. When the film ended, they went back home on foot. It was very dark and nobody else was on the road, so they felt very scared.

听力原文

Ⅲ.

　　Man：What do you think of the concert?

　　Woman：It is awful. The singer didn't do his best.

　　Man：Yep, I find it a little boring. What do you want to do next Saturday?

　　Woman：I prefer to do some outdoor activities rather than go to a cinema or a theatre.

　　Man：Alright, what about having a picnic with our daughters in the park?

　　Woman：That will be great, darling.

·········· Unit 12 ··········

✓ Day 23

Ⅰ.（略）

Ⅱ.

 1. body　　2. head　　3. brain　　4. mouth　　5. neck　　6. arm　　7. stomach

Ⅲ.

1．C   2．A   3．B

Ⅳ．（答案仅供参考）

1．Yes, I have. I had a stomach ache yesterday. It really hurt.

2．Yes, I do. Because a doctor can save many people's lives./No, I don't. Because doctors are so busy and I'm afraid of blood.

3．Last week I didn't get good scores in the English exam so I cried.

听力原文

Ⅲ.

Doctor：Let's check the patient's body. Please tell me some details.

Nurse：OK, doctor. Body temperature is 36 degrees centigrade; the mouth is lightly hurt.

Doctor：What about his head?

Nurse：His head is fine, but you have to look at his stomach.

Doctor：I'm sorry to say that his stomach is badly hurt. However, I believe that he will get better soon.

Nurse：Sure, I'll look after him.

✓ Day 24

Ⅰ．（略）

Ⅱ.

1．face   2．teeth   3．hand   4．leg   5．foot   6．toe

7．medicine   8．smoke   9．headache   10．poor

Ⅲ.

1．A   2．C   3．C

Ⅳ．（答案仅供参考）

When Tom brushed his teeth with a toothbrush, he had a strange feeling in his head. His mother told him that he must have had a cold. So they went to see a doctor. The doctor gave him some medicine against headache. He also told Tom to do more exercise every day to improve his health. The next day, Tom felt better. He wore his sportswear to take exercise outdoors.

听力原文

Ⅲ.

Harry：Hey Jenny, long time no see! What are you doing here?

Jenny：Well, as you can see, I'm doing exercise.

Harry：That's a little strange, because I remember that you don't like any sports, right?

Jenny：No, I hate sports, especially jogging and swimming. And I hate these heavy tools in the gym. I'm doing exercise because my mum asks me to do it…

Harry：Oh Jenny, it is good for your health! Now, as your trainer, I can tell you how to use these tools correctly…

Unit 13

✓ Day 25

Ⅰ．（略）

Ⅱ．

Group 1

1. D 2. A 3. B 4. E 5. C

Group 2

1. E 2. C 3. A 4. B 5. D

Ⅲ．

1. A 2. C 3. B

Ⅳ．（答案仅供参考）

1. I go to school by bus/taxi/boat/tram every day.
2. Yes, I like travelling very much./No, I don't like travelling.
3. I think Disneyland is the most interesting place during my trip.

听力原文

Ⅲ．

1. Mark：Good morning, Richard! Where is your bike? How did you get to school today?
   Richard：Good morning, Mark. My bike broke down on my way to school yesterday and it needed repairing, so I took the bus today.
2. Woman：Excuse me, sir? Which platform does my train leave from? Should I wait here or go to Platform 3?
   Man：Let me have a look at your ticket…We are at Platform 2. Your train will leave from Platform 4. It is at the opposite.
3. Woman：Hi Barb! How was your trip to China?
   Man：It was awesome. We spent four days in Beijing, three days in Shanghai, two days in Xi'an and three days in Chengdu. The people are really nice and I really like Chinese food.

✓ Day 26

Ⅰ．（略）

Ⅱ．

1. zoo 2. elephant 3. dolphin 4. whale 5. campsite
6. ID card 7. station 8. harbour 9. motorway 10. drive

Ⅲ．

1. plane/air 2. zoo 3. campsite

Ⅳ．（答案仅供参考）

Hi, James!

I am going to the zoo with my parents next Saturday. Do you want to join us? I like animals so I am very happy to see them. We will get to the zoo by car. My parents can pick you up.

Best wishes,

(Your name)

听力原文

Ⅲ.

I am Smith and I am planning this year's family trip for my children's summer holiday. We will fly to the destination in the morning and stay at Butterfly Guest-house. For the second day, we will go sightseeing. The city is not big so we can just walk. Eric and Jenny love animals so I will take them to the zoo on the third day. On the fourth day, I will rent a car and drive them to the famous national park. I hope they will find it interesting to stay at the campsite in the forest and be happy to look at the stars at night.

Unit 14

✓ Day 27

Ⅰ.（略）

Ⅱ.

1. talk   2. text   3. call   4. telephone   5. speaker
6. repeat   7. follow   8. share   9. story   10. clear

Ⅲ.

1. B   2. C   3. C

Ⅳ.（答案仅供参考）

1. When I have something happy or unhappy to share with my friends, or when I need their advice on something, I usually chat with them.

2. On weekdays I usually send messages, use voice or video chat on WeChat, or use other chat apps. On weekends I usually meet my friends in some shops or outdoor places to chat with them face to face.

3. I should show my respect for him/her, listen actively, ask questions and repeat, make eye contact and not answer calls or check text messages.

听力原文

Ⅲ.

Marie: Good morning! My name is Marie. Thank you for calling the hotline. How can I help you?

Eric: Good morning, Marie. I'm Eric. I'm calling to ask for some information about the exam for the teacher's certificate.

Marie: Sure. The exams are held in January and July every year. You can sign up for the exam two months in advance. However, for some reason, this year's exam in January was cancelled, and the one in July will be put off.

Eric: I see. It's already May. When can I sign up for the next exam?

Marie: Sorry, Eric. We haven't got any information yet. You can go to our website and get the latest information.

Eric: Okay. Also, how can I sign up for the exam?

Marie: You need to fill up a form online. You can follow the instructions on our website.

✓ Day 28

Ⅰ.（略）

Ⅱ.

Group 1

1. B　　2. C　　3. D　　4. E　　5. A

Group 2

1. B　　2. A　　3. E　　4. C　　5. D

Ⅲ.

1. A　　2. A　　3. B

Ⅳ.（答案仅供参考）

Hello Ryan,

How are you? Haven't seen you for a while! I'm doing great. Our school football team won a match last Saturday and I was really excited. How's your life in the new city? Have you made any new friends? My father bought me a new smartphone, so I can keep in touch with you through phone calls and text messages. Please tell me your phone number.

Best wishes,

(Your name)

听力原文

Ⅲ.

1. Boy: My sister's birthday is coming. I have sent her flowers, books and postcards for her birthdays before. This year I want to prepare a special present for her. Do you have any advice?

   Girl: Um, I guess your sister must like puzzles, because I know she enjoys using her brain.

2. Boy: Excuse me? I want to send a postcard to my friend who lives in Germany. How many stamps should I put on it?

   Woman: To Germany? You can buy a one-dollar stamp. Here it is.

3. Boy: Mrs Simpson, I saw an emoji of a circle with three lines inside. Do you know what it stands for?

   Woman: Oh, that is the symbol of peace. The three lines inside the circle represent letters "N" and "D". Do you want to do some research?